Dr. SHEEHAN
on Running

Dr. SHEEHAN
on Running

by George A. Sheehan M.D.

World Publications

P.O. Box 366
Mountain View, CA 94040

Recommended Reading:
Runner's World Magazine, $9.50/year
Write for a free catalog of publications
and supplies for runners and other athletes.

Illustrated by Bil Canfield
Cover design by Mica Quinn

Contents

Foreword

George Sheehan is a heart specialist, and his patients think he's one of the best. Yet "doctor" is one of the last things I think of when I picture George.

Runner, yes. He's fast enough at the mile to hold a world record for men who've been on this earth 50 or more years. And he's durable enough to race the Boston marathon each spring.

Writer, absolutely. He's good enough to cause *New York Post* columnist Larry Merchant to say, "The best practicing athlete-journalist may be George Sheehan."

Practicing eccentric, to be sure. George, dressed in long-johns and ski mask, once ran past a family moving into his neighborhood. They stared at him. He shouted, "Go back! Everyone in this town is crazy!"

I see George Sheehan lots of ways. But somehow I can't imagine him examining patients. He doesn't fit the white-coat image of a doctor. He shuns the titles, language, appearances and conventions of his profession—dealing, Larry Merchant says, as much with the metaphysical as the physical.

In a field which trains its people in scientific reasoning and laboratory-tested fact, Sheehan is a man who ventures guesses and who trusts what he learns in his "experiment of one." More cautious doctors who read what he writes sometimes criticize him for this. That's okay, he says, because he has criticism for them in return.

He once asked me not to use the letters "M.D." on his non-medical articles. He said, "Some doctors wear the title as if they were born with it."

Another time, he mentioned that most veteran runners know more than most doctors about treating athletic injuries. He said, "The doctor is educated in the treatment of disease, not in health. This is a much more difficult subject. Health is the study of the universe."

George had a conventional medical education. He says he

didn't start learning about true health and fitness until he'd been practicing medicine for 20-odd years. And he didn't learn it then from medical texts, but from becoming a runner.

Running has been his own experiment of one. He has learned to treat athletic injuries by treating his own. And running has radically changed his views of man's physical potential and of aging. More than this, though, it has helped him find the person he always wanted to be and was meant to be.

"Running,'" he has written, "frees me from the monosyllabic inanities of my usual tongue-tied state, liberates me from the polysyllabic jargon of my profession, removes me from the kind of talk which aims at concealing rather than revealing what is in my heart, and what I mean to do and be."

George Sheehan was meant to write, and we were fated to get together. I was a new editor of *Runner's World* magazine in 1970, and George was fairly new to running and writing. I can't remember which of us asked the other about writing for *RW*, but George said, "Ask for readers' medical questions and I'll answer them. Print some of the better ones." His "Medical Advice" column was in the first issue I edited, and has been in ever since.

Letters now come in at the rate of 10-25 a week, and George answers all of them personally . . . plus writing a weekly column for a newspaper (the *Red Bank Register*) in the New Jersey town where he practices. Most of the essays in this book originally appeared in the *Register*.

George lives across the country from me, and I've only seen him twice in recent years. I hear from him by letter or phone almost every work day. But only twice have we gotten together to talk. Both times, he was speaking at sports medicine seminars.

At the first one, he said, "I'm not here as a doctor but as an athletes' representative." And he talked athlete-to-athlete and athlete-to-doctor, not doctor-to-doctor.

I noticed then how little importance he gives to appearances. He wore a faded blue shirt with a frayed, button-down collar. His narrow tie was held in place by a paper clip.

Two years later, he wrote, "I now wear skin-tight Levis, over-the-calf hose, some old running shoes and a cotton turtle-neck shirt. Anything added to this is simply for concealment."

He didn't conceal anything when he spoke the second time. He'd lost his reading glasses ($2 Woolworth's specials), and so he spoke without notes. The talk was to be on the heart abnormalities of athletes, but he barely brushed that subject. Instead, he spun out the Sheehan Philosophy—the same kind of philosophical, personal messages he writes here. The audience, somewhat numbed by a day and a half of clinical lectures, loved what George said.

Obviously, there are many truths in what he says, because George Sheehan is one of the most quoted men in running. Few people have more of an influence on the present generation of athletes.

Frank Shorter, the Olympic marathon champion, paid George something of a compliment when he complained about conversations with some runners. He said, "I don't want to talk about Dr. Sheehan all the time."

George isn't for everyone, but his writing does have a wide appeal. Several years ago, George phrased what might have been an answer to Shorter and a statement to his own potential readers:

"For every runner who tours the world running marathons, there are thousands who run to hear the leaves and listen to rain and look to the day when it all is suddenly as easy as a bird in flight. For them, sport is not a test but a therapy, not a trial but a reward, not a question but an answer."

Joe Henderson

Notes and Quotes

My family rarely gives me any credit for original thought. When a topic comes under discussion at the dinner table, someone is likely to turn to me and ask, "What would Bucky Fuller say about that?" Or from the end of the table comes the query, "Any words from the Greek philosophers?"

And as with most things said in jest to a friend, or in anger to an enemy, or in drink to no one in particular, these questions have the ring of truth. I am living proof that you can go through the world on borrowed words. Whatever happens, there seems to be someone who has already expressed my reaction to the event much better than I could. So I find it difficult to speak without giving voice to someone else's words.

I have found a company of these "someones" who have given voice to exactly how I feel, only have done it much better and clearer than I. People like James and Ortega and Santayana and Fuller and a few Greeks. I quote them because they said so well what *I* was thinking. They described my experience, my personal truth, in miraculously right words.

But a fundamental fact of nature is that no man can understand for another. We can amass quantities of ideas and philosophies. But it is just so much trivia unless it is in some way materialized. The great teacher, said Santayana, is matter. The world teaches, not books.

"Anyone who has had a bull by the tail," observed Mark Twain, "knows five or six things more than someone who hasn't."

"Culture," wrote Father Gannon after surveying the effect of his years as president of Fordham University, "is what is left when everything you have been taught is forgotten."

What you have left are phrases and disconnected sayings of famous men, the giants on whose shoulders we stand sayings that pop into our minds and onto our tongues in day-to-day situations. One hardly knows why.

These quotations are filled with wisdom. But as Bergan Evans points out in the preface to his book of quotations, "Wisdom is meaningless unless our own experience gives it meaning."

Wisdom, then, is the incorporation of the thoughts of others into our own experience—the ability to see someone else's truth and see that you share it. It is not enough to know the great thinkers, the great writers, the great poets. You must find those who approximate your existence, your contact with the universe.

Wherever you arrive, you will find they have been there first and described it better. This should not discourage you. You should let your own juices flow. Hope for a minor miracle of your own. Perhaps then you can contribute your own awareness for others to share.

With help from my old friends, I hope I can contribute a few original thoughts here, as springboards for your own thinking.

*"Life is a desperate struggle
to succeed in being in fact
that which we are in design."*
—Ortega y Gasset

Part I

THE RUNNER

One

Myself and Yourself

At the age of reason, I was placed on a train, the shades drawn, my life's course and destination already determined. At the age of 45, I pulled the emergency cord and ran out into the world. It was a decision that meant no less than a new life, a new course, a new destination. I was born again in my 45th year.

The previous "me" was not me. It was a self-image I had thrust upon me. It was the person I had accepted myself to be, but I had been playing a role.

"It took me a long time to discover that the key to acting is honesty," an actor told anthropologist Edmund Carpenter. "Once you know how to fake that, you've got it made."

In time, we fool even ourselves. Sooner or later, however, we come to question the trip planned for us, the goals we are given, our itinerary to death. Sooner or later, the self-image becomes not worth preserving. The person we are presumed to be seems unsatisfactory and inadequate. Sooner or later, it becomes important that we feel important and have the feeling that what we are doing is important.

When I stepped off that train, I had lost my sense of purpose, my faith in what I was doing, my caring for creation and its creatures. And when I stepped from that train, I found I was not alone. Millions of Americans who had been told Sunday after Sunday to be born again were now going through the shattering experience of rebirth. Only the experts don't call it that. They call it "middle-aged melancholia," or a "new cultural phenomenon of the fourth and fifth decade," or more simply "change of life."

The authorities agree that we come upon this stage of our life unprepared for the reality of advancing years and receding rewards. White-collar worker, blue-collar worker, housewife and career woman, no one seems immune to the crisis that sets in after the 40s get under way. Each of us in our own way comes to this revelation and faces the problem of living according to the person we really are.

This is not only inevitable, it is desirable. "He who does not really feel himself lost," wrote Ortega, "is lost beyond remission. He never finds himself, never comes up against his own reality."

Finding one's reality does not come without plan or effort. Being born again is no easy task. Technique and training and much hard work are needed. And we are always faced with the knowledge that it is an undertaking that will never be completed. Every day will be a fresh start.

Most experts suggest we make a new start in a new career, develop new interests. I say begin at the beginning. Begin with the body. The body mirrors the soul and the mind, and is much more accessible than either. Become proficient at listening to your body and you will eventually hear from your totality—the complex, unique person you are.

I did it that way. I stepped off that train and began to run. And in that hour a day of perfecting my body, I began to find out who I was. I discovered that my body was a marvelous thing, and learned that any ordinary human can move in ways that have excited painters and sculptors since time began. I didn't need the scientists to tell me that man is a microcosm of the universe, that he contains the 92 elements of the cosmos in his body. In the creative action of running, I became convinced of my own importance, certain that my life had significance.

Fitness may have something to do with this. The physiologists have shown us that those who remain the perpetual athlete are two and even three decades younger physically than their contemporaries. And with this comes an awareness, a physical intelligence, a sensual connection with everything around you that enlarges your existence.

If decreases in the body's functions are due to non-use and not to aging, is it unreasonable to suggest that our mental and psychological and spiritual capabilities deteriorate the same way?

If so, our rebirth will be a long and difficult task. It will begin with the creative use of the body, in the course of which we must explore pain and exhaustion as closely as pleasure and satisfaction. It will end only when we have stretched our minds and souls just as far.

But there is an alternative. You can always get back on the train.

The trouble with you, Doc, is that you're assimilated," a friend told me. "You've forgotten you're Irish."

He was partly right. I have forgotten I am Irish. I still have the underdog mentality that is part of the Irish mystique. (Like the Jews and Southerners, the Irish have made a career out of losing.) And a returning tourist once told me she had seen my eyes all over Connemara. But I no longer consider myself Irish. I no longer hear that ethnic tune.

But I have not been assimilated. I know now I am part of another distinct group—the distance runners. It took me a decade or more of running to realize I had been born with the mind and heart and body of a runner. I share this peculiarity with distance runners all over the world. We have some unique somatotype—a blend of bone and muscle and nervous tissue that makes running what we do best.

"The somatotype," wrote Shelton in his classical study *The Atlas of Man,* "identifies a person as belonging to a biological group or family which appears to be worldwide in distribution." These body types, he says, therefore cut across the uncertain borders by which men have attempted to divide themselves—like race and color and blood-type and geography.

I belong to the distance running family. Double my height in inches and you have my weight. My bones are small, my legs relatively short. My muscles are stringy, and I have little body fat. Like my fellows, I tend to be a solitary person and more of a thinker than a doer. But since we must find some action and physical expression, we find it in running.

The reason for this is apparently our economy of movement against gravity. Nature always moves in the direction of accomplishing more and more with less and less energy. And the runner can go farther on less energy than almost any animal on earth.

Why should I be something as incidental as Irish when I can be something as basic and fundamental as a runner? As a runner, I live totally. My every waking hour is lived as a runner. I eat as a runner. I view the weather, the terrain, the environment as a runner. I see all things as positive or negative in their action on my running. All of this happens because my body type is the most deep-seated, most general and most evident expression of what kind of person I am.

Running, however restricted it appears to viewers, is my mode of self-expression. Running is for me a subject of study that need never end. And within its confines I must work out my salvation.

We distance runners are meditative men. If we have a religious tradition, it is one of non-conformity and withdrawal, the hermit, the anchorite. At best, we hope for a secluded meadow where we won't be disturbed.

Given society's emphasis on the values of community and helping our fellow man, we distance runners have difficulty comprehending that what we do is exactly right for us. At such times, I like to recall that Thoreau—another confirmed loner—once said that there was nothing more important to him than his walks, and he had no walks to throw away on company.

Every distance runner knows that feeling.

U ntil I took up distance running, I found it easy to take it easy. I had no difficulty following the warnings of the experts. "Avoid stress," cautioned the physicians. I did. "Reduce your tensions," advised the psychologists. I did. "Rest that restless heart," counseled the clergy. I did.

Doing these things requires no effort when you are lacking what Santayana called America's ruling passion—a love for business—when you are a lifelong non-joiner whose greatest desire is not to become involved, when almost everyone you meet is less interesting than your own ideas, and when your inner life has more reality than your outer one.

Running has not changed that. I am still a small-boned loner built for flight and fantasy. I cannot manufacture an interest or talent for business or institutions or people. Beyond these limitations, however, I now accept no limitations.

It may be common sense for the common man to consent to be ordinary. But now everything instinctive, everything intuitive, everything beyond logic tells me otherwise. It tells me that compared to what I ought to be, I am only half awake. It tells me that, as William James did, I am using only a small part of my mental and physical resources. Running gave me these insights. It made me an athlete, albeit an aging one, and started my ascent toward a new goal.

Now I accept stress, and even seek it out. I no longer avoid the tension between what I am and what I perceive I can be. I no longer ignore the gap between what I have achieved and what I should accomplish. I realize that I have yet to live the perfect day, the day worthy of reliving. And I know Maslow was right when he suggested that equilibrium and adaptation and self-preservation and adjustment are negative concepts.

When I run my hour on the roads, I accept no negatives. I may start with a leisurely pace, but soon the hills come and I must attack them. Every hill is a challenge. No pain, no shortness of breath will stop me until I reach the top completely spent. And even then I wish the hill would go still higher.

Surely this is a mad act. Health doesn't demand this. Health is, in fact, something passed through on the way to this seemingly unnecessary area of fitness. This area is also quite dangerous because just beyond the possibility of doing as well as I am able lies the dread condition of overtraining, with its exhaustion and fatigue, its apathy and depression. And just as stress on the body can affect both heart and head, so the tension that upsets the psyche takes a similar toll on the body.

But if these dangers exist, the converse is also true. When you complete yourself physically, it benefits you totally. And the energies exist to accomplish this. The real problem is to discover how these energy reserves can be set loose.

My method is running. It is the hub of my creative wheel. At those moments, I am athlete, poet, philosopher, even saint. Running introduces risk, and takes me beyond tranquility and harmony and the smooth workings of ordinary day-to-day living. When I run, I recognize my essential inadequacy, my insufficiency of body, mind and heart. And I realize the only answer is in pushing myself to the limits on the roads, or in struggling for the right word to express the truth, or in searching for meaning for myself and the universe.

Still, the experts may be right. Stress is a killer. Tensions do cause neuroses. Uneasiness of the heart can lead to despair. But without them, we remain inferior to our true selves. Live if you will a life without risk. Avoid the forge, the fire, the flame. But know that joy and happiness and the good life come only as unexpected interludes in the endless, stressful, tense and restless journey to become the person you are.

There is no easy way.

When I began running in my mid-40s, I rewrote my life story. It has become a biography of pain. I have made a career out of suffering. I've discovered that the middle-aged person is the perfect laboratory animal for research in sports medicine. Whatever happens to an athlete will happen first to a middle-aged athlete.

Scientific progress was not my original intention. Fun was, and fitness, and perhaps achievement. I hoped to acquire the look and moves and self-confidence of the athlete—to be sleek, quick and instinctive. There might even be a glorious reprise to a not-so-glorious collegiate record.

But I soon learned that injury was to be the dominant theme of my new vocation. "Running hurt" became commonplace. The fun was there, and so was the fitness, plus meditation

and other values I had not suspected. But I was neither sleek nor quick nor instinctive. I was ragged and slow and uncoordinated, more often limping than not.

As time passed and my mileage grew, I developed every runner's injury in the books, and some that weren't. I went through a cram course in sports medicine. Instead of reading about diseases, I got them. I became a mobile medical museum.

Eventually, I took a biblical approach to these afflictions. The cause of man's infirmity is to be found in man himself. Germs and microbes were not the problem. No virus had produced these miseries. I was dealing with a loss of the body's integrity, its balance, its ability to remain in equilibrium with its environment, its capacity to cope.

My little disasters, my minor tragedies became opportunities to find that integrity, that balance and the antidote to the stress of training. I began to ask questions and find some answers: answers to metatarsalgia and plantar fasciitis, to achilles tendinitis and pseudo-achilles tendinitis, to heel spurs and shin splints, to runner's knee and groin pulls, to stress fractures and sciatic neuritis.

Some lasted longer than others and gave me a better education. Four years of sciatica taught me how to sleep (on my good side with my bad leg drawn up), how to drive a car (only in bucket seats), how to sit (with the hips higher than the knees), how to have patience ("I had it for two years once," an older runner told me). I am a powerfully slow learner, but I began to learn.

Every painful mile I put on the roads adds more of this kind of information, but I still have trouble welcoming injury. When it arrives, I still go through that familiar sequence of every patient: disbelief, followed by fear, then rage and finally depression.

I should, however, have a lot of time to work on that problem. After all, whatever happens to an athlete will happen first to an 80-year-old athlete.

Should you meet me, don't ask me how I am. A half-hour later, you are likely to be glancing at your watch, shifting from one foot to the other and clearing your throat trying to interrupt a monologue of my symptoms. By that time, I will have covered my troubles with my feet and knees and low back. I will have reported on my sinuses and bronchial tubes and my nasal allergies. I will have described in great detail my intestinal malfunctions.

But whatever the inventory of miseries you hear before you escape, it will list only the more superficial of my problems. Your question goes beyond blemishes. It encompasses my whole person and demands a total answer.

How am I? You have set in motion a self-examination that can only end in my getting suited up and racing against the clock at the local track. The real answer must be found in action, and in reaction to maximum physical and psychological stress.

How am I? Until I'm asked, I'm able to keep my mind off it. I live in my fantasy world. I avoid reality by day-dreaming. What else can a small-boned distance runner with an oversupply of nerve endings and no fat to insulate him do about reality? Think about it as little as possible is the obvious answer.

A person with my body build and temperament, as all psychiatrists know, is relatively hypochondriacal, dependent, passive, unhappy and psychologically vulnerable. The best way to cope with that is withdrawal. So when someone asks me how I am, my defense is shattered.

How am I? Oddly, that question is much more disturbing if I feel well. That is a clear indication things are going wrong. I have yet to meet a runner who admitted to feeling well before he ran a good race. The conversation at the starting line of almost any distance race would give you the impression you were in a doctor's waiting room. Hardly a runner is present who hasn't complaints of such magnitude you wonder how he made it to the race, or indeed why he even left his sick-bed.

And it is always those who feel the worst—the ones with the casts and tape and bandages, the ones who have been up all night with diarrhea—who disappear ahead of you the second the gun sounds. The next time you see them, they have already finished and are in their sweat clothes cheering you on. The race has been a remarkable therapy for them. They had a miraculous cure.

How am I? The race is the answer, the only answer. The runner is truly a man dissatisfied with the status quo. His object is to reach goals that are continually being reset. And he is only aware of where he is and who he is when he is challenged. Like the saint, he is everlastingly beset by doubt and just as everlastingly asking to be tested.

So don't ask me how I am. And one other thing. Don't tell me I look well. Runners who look well are at least five pounds overweight, and are on their way to being happy and contented and psychologically invulnerable. I want no part of that.

Two

Fitness and Fun

Dr. Thomas Tutko, the sports psychologist, was asked by a fitness instructor how to decide which sport a student should be in.

"Just ask him," said Tutko. "Have the student rate the activities on a scale of five (like very much) to one (dislike very much)."

Until I heard that answer, I had supposed that students could be tested to find their sports—that measurement of body types, plus determinations of coordination, strength and flexibility could be added to psychological testing and fed into a computer. The computer would then deliver the exact sport for each person.

Now Tutko was giving us the same answer Greeks got at Delphi—an answer repeated by sages ever since. "Know thyself" is the cryptic message. We must find our own answers, find our own sport. The wise man tells us how to find our own wisdom. He cannot give us his.

All this is maddening to those of us who wish to confer happiness to others, to lead their lives for them and tell them what's best. And it's perhaps even more maddening to those of us who would have our future determined by some omnipotent counselor. It is no wonder that Athenians, looking for answers, turned on Socrates when he replied by telling them to examine their lives.

How can a student rate a sport he has never experienced? He can't. That is just the point. How can a person find out whether paddleball is his game, whether archery is his thing, if scuba diving will turn him on, if any one of a number of sports give him what the late Abraham Maslow called a peak experience—"a moment when a person's powers are at their height and he becomes a spontaneous, coordinated, efficient organism functioning with a great flow of power that is so peculiarly effortless that it may become like play—masterful, virtuoso-like"?

Tutko says we will find that peak experience only by experiencing it. We will learn this most difficult lesson in the world, as Goethe said, never by thinking but by doing.

We may be helped, however, if we know what kind of person selects a particular sport. If the man who gets his peak experience running marathons matches you in temperament and personality, the odds are your unifying activity will be marathon-like sport. This at least reduces the Tutko injunction to something manageable. The number of sports to be experienced is cut down to a reasonable number.

Something of this sort is being tested in a nationwide career program. It consists of exposing the student to 20,000 different types of jobs. The jobs are grouped into 15 clusters which are classified as "the world of manufacturing," "the world of construction," etc. The children in grades 7-9 are given actual experiences in one or more of these job clusters. They explore them in depth. In construction, for instance, they investigate the work of the architect, engineer, craftsman.

Dr. Sidney High, who is managing the program, says, "I've never seen so little money spent to trigger so much response." That response may well represent a recognition that the individual must ultimately be his own judge and save his own life.

That life will be ideally an inextricable mix of vocation and avocation—a career which meshes with and is complemented by athletic activity. To achieve this, schools must not only provide career awareness but athletic awareness. There should not only be job clusters but sports clusters where the students will find what they do best.

What we are looking for are those activities in which a student displays skill, confidence and creativeness. How do we know? "Ask him," says Dr. Tutko.

Despite our multimillion-dollar "health services" bill, the United States is the best place to be if you are sick—but one of the last places to be if you wish to remain well. Recent statistics show that the overfed, underexercised United States is 37th in life expectancy for men 40 years of age. (We were 11th two decades earlier.) Further, our women have a 6.8 years greater life expectancy than our men at that age, against 3.4 years in the leading countries.

People who planned to do something about this formed the National Jogging Association in the late 1960s. The NJA was the brainchild of Lt. Gen. R.L. Bohannon M.D., who boosted jogging as "the simplest, cheapest, least encumbered, most available and most efficient way to build up the heart and lungs."

Gen. Bohannon looked for little or no help from the medical profession, which he said had failed to recognize the current health gap—"the gap between absence of disease on the one hand and true *joie de vivre* with all its energy, vitality and well-being on the other."

The general then spelled out a program of eight minutes calisthenics warmup, 20 minutes of walking-jogging or jogging, followed by a cooldown of five minutes of walking—all of this to be done three times a week. "It is time," he said, "for every American to ascertain his proper program and get with it." However, the NJA has never had more than a few thousand members.

Another military man, Air Force doctor Kenneth Cooper, spread the jogging message in the late '60s and the effect was almost revolutionary. Publication of his book *Aerobics* in 1968 set millions of people to jogging. But many, if not most, dropped out after a few days or weeks.

Dr. Cooper, a by-the-numbers researcher, did a prodigious amount of work on the effects of exercise. He documented its benefits to the heart, lungs and muscles. He even systematized the relationship between muscular effort and future health. He said, "I'm practicing preventive medicine."

This methodical, scientific approach has given his book a solid foundation—solid enough to convince him that every American should follow his program. Obviously, not every American has followed it. Cooper, according to *Time* magazine, has enlisted eight million citizens in his program of graduated exercises (mostly jogging) designed to protect against heart-artery disease and prevent premature death. But these figures must include anyone caught on the street after curfew or noticed inquiring the way to the nearest YMCA.

I suspect that "aerobics" has not had more converts because Cooper seems to view fitness in a vacuum. Cooper's tables measure, as Bobby Kennedy once said of the Gross National Product, everything except what makes life worthwhile. The GNP, said Kennedy, can tell us everything except why we are proud to be Americans. Cooper's stats tell us everything except why people run and cycle and swim and enjoy using their bodies.

That, of course, is the key. And until Cooper and others interested in the preservation and perfection of the body spell this out, we will make little progress.

They are, you see, relying on individual conversions. And even Bucky Fuller, possibly the world's greatest optimist, has little faith in changing man. Change his environment, Fuller advises. It can be done without that, of course, but only by the way we are protected against small pox and polio. By force. Shots for everyone will become athletics for everyone, and in doses recommended by medical authorities. Attention America! Now run, jump, do anything to raise your pulse to 120 beats for 30 minutes a week.

But there is an alternative to the athletic-state or the exercise-your-heart-ailments-away argument of the aerobics plan. The answer is to consult your friendly neighborhood athlete, be he runner, tennis player, or overaged half-court basketball player. Why does he do it?

A composite of this latter-day athlete would show him to be little different from everyone else on the block. The future concerns him little. He is practically and philosophically a "to-

day" person, a member of the "now" generation, whatever his age. Instant gratification is his mark.

This guy has discovered the truth of Brian Glanville's statement: "If you do not exercise the body, it corrupts—and the mind corrupts with it."

The neighborhood athlete is willing to let you in on the secret. Running pays off, and it pays off today. Exercise gives instant and exhilarating effects. There is a natural high to be obtained legally.

But to have this, we must tailor the addiction to the addict. Pick his sport according to his body build, his psychological needs and the demands of his culture. The 5'6", 130-pound loner will find satisfaction where the corpulent, gregarious *bon vivant* would go nuts. The broad-shouldered, well-muscled extrovert is in a different category yet.

Some people need contests which are essentially a struggle with self, and others need games which are a classroom in interpersonal relationships. And those games may have to be games of chance or skill or strategy, depending on the individual. This complexity should not worry us, for it explains our failures and points the way to a rational plan for everyone to adopt.

Armed with this, Dr. Cooper could offer the athletic equivalent of the Vermont Alternative suggested by ex-New Yorker Bill Allen. "It offers," wrote Allen about Vermont, "an oasis of sanity and survival in a world full of suffering, cruelty and chaos . . . and an answer to the question of the 1970s: 'Is there life after birth?' Not frenetic or freakout life, but close to the heart's desire and a kind of grace beyond confusion."

Play and games and sport offer the same oasis. Only nonathletes will consider this an exaggeration.

Will jogging be only a temporary insanity like hula-hoops, the twist and psychoanalysis? Such an opinion was advanced not long ago in a "Talk of the Town" column of the *New Yorker*.

"Jogging is a pastime of overpowering ennui," according to this urbane commentator who sees only ultimate boredom for the jogger, followed by a return to a "short snooze, a martini, and the evening news."

To those of us who are mainline joggers and get withdrawal symptoms if we go more than 48 hours without running, such opinions seem incredible. And to compare our consuming avocation adversely with golf and tennis because we lack the "coordination and physical skills to pursue these difficult, interesting sports without embarrassment" is to miss entirely the total involvement of running.

This is not to say that there won't be dropouts, and many of them, from the jogging program. Chesterton wrote that you should never do anything "merely because it is good for you." Those who do will invariably be found out and will return to more palatable pursuits.

For those who endure, running will bring those values sought by all men: the habit of contemplation developed in solitary long runs, the art of conversation found again in running with a companion, the sense of community born in the communal anticipation, agony and eventual relaxation of the competitive race, and finally the development of maximum physical capabilities which in turn help us to find our maximum spiritual and intellectual potential.

This is no small package. And if the *New Yorker* essayist sees only boredom on the faces of the joggers he observes, it is because he views the harried look of the average urban dweller as normal. What the jogger's face shows is not boredom but contemplation, which Thomas Aquinas described as man's highest activity save one—contemplation plus putting the fruits of that contemplation into action.

Be assured that true joggers will not be deterred by the *New Yorker* article any more than our forebears were discouraged a century ago by the editorial in *Scientific American* which accused oarsmen and long distance walkers of "pleading the old cant of promotion of health and all the rest of it," and warned that these activities would not be beneficial.

We do indeed plead the old cant of health, but are even more concerned about "all the rest of it"—i.e., the contemplation, conversation and community that this activity offers.

J oggers May Be Running to an Early Grave"
Faced with a headline like that, what do you do? Read the article, certainly. So now you know that some San Francisco researchers have compiled reports on sudden deaths from coronary artery disease and found that more than half of them occurred during moderate to strenuous activity. Now what do you do? To jog or not to jog, that is the question.

Intellect, reason, intuition should go into that decision. How can I be the best possible me? What is the only possible life for me to lead? Can all this be accomplished without daily and vigorous exercise?

I doubt it. I also feel the dangers of strenuous exercise have been exaggerated, its value underrated. Any number of studies have shown that people who exercise regularly have fewer heart attacks than those who don't. Studies have also demonstrated that regular exercisers have a substantially better chance of surviving a heart attack should they have one.

In a three-year Health Insurance Plan of New York study of 110,000 people, physically active men had only one-half the number of heart attacks of the inactive men, and in the most active men only one-eighth the number of deaths.

Such results have been repeated recently in a survey of 17,000 civil servants in England. There, in men reporting vigorous activity, the relative risk of developing coronary disease was about a third of that in men who did not exercise.

Further, the more active one is, the greater the protection. Dr. Thomas Bassler, editor of the American Medical Joggers Association bulletin, states that mileage is the best protection. He says he has yet to find a marathoner of any age having a fatal coronary attack.

Dr. Richard Steiner, a pathologist-marathoner, says, "Long distance running can give you a teenage cholesterol, remodel your lungs, lower your blood pressure and slow your pulse."

On top of that, the jogger-runner stops smoking, loses weight and develops a relaxed, playful approach toward the absurdities of everyday existence. Distance running, the additive that cleans his arteries, also cleans his mind and soul.

Seen in this light, daily vigorous exercise is needed for the actual as well as the potential coronary victim. Heart disease is, if anything, more an indication *for* exercise than not.

"Stress tests," says Per-Olof Astrand, perhaps the world's best-known exercise physiologist, "should be reserved for those who won't exercise." Then they would know, he declares, whether they are in good enough health to stand a sedentary life.

Still, exercise is not without danger. Neither is driving a car and crossing a street. You learn to exercise defensively just as you learn to drive defensively. You don't attack exercise with a stopwatch and measured miles.

"There is no evidence that speed protects," says Dr. Bassler, "but mileage does."

Pace, then, is paramount. Dr. Thomas Cureton has taken 12,000 people through his fitness course without a fatality. He simply uses common sense: a suitable warmup (up to 20 minutes) to allow the body's physiology to accommodate to its function, and then a pace which the body can handle on a pay-as-you-go, aerobic basis.

The idea that pace is unique for each person goes back to Galen, the medical advisor to Marcus Aurelius. Writing about ball-playing, he said it was the best exercise for the body and lungs, and the most vigorous of all sports. He warned, however, that "the right degree must be found in practice. It cannot be expressed in writing."

Our present-day English translation of that rule is Bill Bowerman's "talk test." Jog or run, says Bowerman, at a pace at which you can converse with a companion. If a slow jog is still too fast for conversation, you have to start with a walk instead.

If you follow this advice, you will have come upon what Francis Bacon called for almost four centuries ago: "A safe, convenient and civil way to prolong and renew life."

Most recreational directors, physical education instructors, and promoters of exercise-for-your-health programs feel much the same as the fellow who finds it difficult to give away five-dollar bills down Main Street. People just won't believe it's for real.

The programs they prescribe seem so sensible and so in keeping with our nature it is incredible that people don't accept them. But facts are facts and there is no use railing against them. If the plane won't fly, there's no use appealing that the blueprints said it would. A bridge that insists on collapsing in defiance to all engineering theory will not respond to oaths and imprecations. Nor will our neighbors bestir themselves to physical activity unless we find the proper approach to the problem.

Threats fail. Horror stories of future heart attacks, diabetes and strokes have predictably fallen on deaf ears. People are not inclined to do something just because it is good for them. Athletics in schools should be chosen on the basis of what the teachers would like to do themselves. This is the rule followed by James Herndon, author of *How to Survive in Your Native Land*. What you don't do, the students won't do, was what Herndon found out.

"Why should we assume that the kids would want to do a lot of stuff that we didn't want to do, and wouldn't ever do of our own free will?" he asks. "Does the math teacher go home at night and do a few magic squares? Does the English teacher go home at night and diagram sentences?"

What about the physical education teacher? What about the other teachers? Can't they bring to the student the vitality of the drama, the esthetics that they themselves get out of the sport? Can we find coaches who can make lifelong athletes out of their students?

We have forgotten that we are talking about play. We are dealing with one of the primary categories of life, one which resists all logical interpretation. Play has a deeper basis than utility. It exists of and for itself.

When we expose play to the function of promoting fitness and preventing heart attacks, we change its gold to dross. As countless fairy tales have told us, the choice of treasure over truth will always fail. What we need then is to conserve those mysterious and elusive elements of play which make it its own reward. We must remove anything that suggests practicality and usefulness. What we do must be fun and impractical and useless, or else we won't do it. If we become fit and impervious to heart attacks and all those other dread diseases, it will be because we don't care if we drop dead doing what we like to do.

We should be in sports not because they are practical but because they're not, not because we feel better but because we don't care how we feel, not because our fitness is increased but because we are so interested we don't even notice.

Play is the key. We all love to play. We like only the jobs that have a play element for us. Anything as practical as physical education or physical fitness is not going to get to first base with most of us.

Three

Running and Walking

Why is running the best exercise?
1. It is the easiest to do. Running requires a minimum of equipment, no companions and no athletic ability. It can be done almost any time and any place.

2. It is a physiologically perfect exercise. Running uses the large thigh and leg muscles in rhythmic fashion at a personally controlled rate. This is the requirement for safely developing cardiopulmonary function.

3. It has predictably good results on the body and mind. Running has been proven to (a) increase cardiopulmonary fitness, (b) reduce weight, (c) lower blood pressure, (d) decrease the cholesterol and triglycerides associated with coronary disease, and (e) help psychological stability.

Why is running not the best exercise?

Only 10-15% of people are natural runners who will stick to it. Others who are more athletic and muscular will run only as part of another sport. Those who tend to be more broad than long will not run at all. Sport to them is walking, cycling, skating, skiing or swimming.

How will I know if running is my exercise?

If you ran in school, tend to be narrow rather than wide, have small wrists and weigh in pounds twice your height in inches, you will probably like to run. If you are a loner, have few friends and have been described as a dreamer, you can go out and buy your shoes right now.

What shoes should I use?

Shoes are the runner's only significant expense, and should be good ones. Each major brand (Adidas, New Balance, Nike, Puma, Tiger, etc.) puts out a good training shoe. What you look for is a good-sized heel with a strong heel counter, a multi-layered sole (to handle shock) and a solid shank. The ones I have used and recommend are the Puma 9190, Adidas Country, Nike Cortez or Tiger Corsair and the New Balance Trackster III.

What clothes should I wear?

Winter training requires a base of long-johns or thermal underwear. Over this, cotton turtleneck shirts are usually enough, although a light nylon rain jacket also may be needed. Avoid bulky garments. Use several light layers instead. A wool ski mask and thermal mittens or socks for the hands complete the outfit. In the summer, cotton shirts should be worn and nylon avoided. For socks, the best are the tennis anklets now available with and without pompons.

How should I regulate my diet?

Solids should be avoided for 2-3 hours before running. In very hot weather, 10 ounces of one of the "Ade" drinks should be taken within 10 minutes of the start and every 20 minutes thereafter. Fluids with a high concentration of sugar should be taken well diluted. Otherwise, they will cause loss of fluid into the gut and bring on diarrhea.

How should I start my running program?

Running, whether you are in your first day or 10th year, should be done at a conversational pace—a speed at which you can talk with a companion. And the first 10 minutes should be even slower to allow you to reach your second wind. In the beginning, this may mean only a brisk walk or at best the old reliable scout pace—50 paces walking, alternating with 50 paces jogging. As time goes by, the effort will remain the same, but your minutes per mile will improve steadily.

How far should I run?

Lifetime runners should not be concerned with speed or distance. Runners deal in moderate effort (determined by the "talk test") over increasing periods of time. Start with 5-10 minutes every other day and work up to 30 minutes 3-4 times a week. This will achieve most of the results enumerated in question one.

What injuries can I expect, and how can I prevent them?

Ninety-five percent of runners' overuse injuries (stress fracture, heel spur, runner's knee, etc.) are due to weak feet plus muscle imbalance. Running shortens the calf, hamstring and low-back muscles, and it also causes relative weakening of the abdominal muscles. Support for the feet and daily exercises should give you permanent pain-free running.

What is gained by running more than 1½-2 hours a week?

A good question. Dr. Thomas Bassler of the American Medical Joggers Association states that only by running an hour a day six days a week can you become immune to coronary disease. However, one who embarks on these efforts tends to leave other loyalties behind. He becomes a completely new person living a completely new life-style. Whether this is good or ill is at all times debatable. Running can break up families, destroy friendships and kill ambition. It can also, of course, rebuild families, create new friendships and inspire ambition.

Take a 30-60-minute run every other day. On the off days, try to fit in token 15-minute workouts. And if a leg or muscle injury develops, take a daily 30-minute swim until the injury disappears.

Sound impossible, or if possible something which only top-notch long distance runners would attempt? Not at all. Each day before or after work, thousands of individuals put on a sweat suit and a pair of sneakers or running shoes and take to the roads or country for an exhilarating jaunt. Although many of these runners are in training for weekend long distance races, the majority forget about the word training and are out for the fun of it. It's amazing how the miles click by, especially if you're running with a partner. I myself adhere to the 30-60-minute sessions and find that in addition to the fun aspect, the workouts lead to a slimmer figure, toned-up muscles, lower blood pressure, better sleep, greater work production and more relaxation.

I don't suppose that the above benefits do much in the way of recruiting new members into the ranks of long distance runners. For the man who has done little in the way of activity after leaving the high school or college gym, the thought of running for 30-60 minutes straight is overwhelming—no matter what the rewards. Yet, what we are looking at in myself and others who do run long distances every day is the end product of a program which may have started with a daily 10-minute walk mixed with slow jogging. Many people are already doing that without realizing that they're on the first leg of what could become a daily 10-15-mile run. Why not find a walking or jogging partner in your neighborhood? You may find out that with time you will be running partners.

Starting a personal program of endurance training means following one general rule: "Train, don't strain." For example, don't make the mistake of running up grades in the early sessions. I made that mistake. My over-enthusiasm resulted in a pull of the gastrocnemius muscle and my longest disability of four weeks.

The neophyte should start slowly by alternately walking and jogging a quarter-mile and then gradually building up to a mile after a period of about two weeks. At this point, start jogging a mile at a speed which would permit you to talk easily with a running companion. That pace may turn out to be quite slow for the first six to nine minutes, or until a "second wind" develops. Signalled by the onset of sweating and a slowing of the respiratory rate, this new burst of energy or second wind will mean that you can try longer distances.

Running until the second wind develops is a sort of warmup exercise which signifies an ability of endurance. Elite athletes reach that stage in three minutes, but personally I feel it after six minutes like clockwork. Then I shift into high gear and start thinking of running 20 miles. However, this feeling of euphoria gradually fades as you put on running mileage. And then when you think you just can't run another inch—after about 35 or 40 minutes—you get another lift which keeps you going for another 10-20 minutes.

Adolph Gruber, an Austrian long distance champion, once told me that anyone could run a marathon by observing this rule: "Hold back for the first seven miles, use it as a warmup, and then gradually increase your rate but never strain." For the person just starting out, however, seven miles is in itself a marathon. But here's some good news. Few of even the experienced runners try the marathon and most are content to get the physical and mental and spiritual benefit from an ordinary 30-60 minutes of motion.

Another trick to keep interest high in the early stages of a running program is to select different running routes. Bill Bowerman, who has been so successful in coaching track at Oregon University, has five or six different cross-country courses for his runners. Running the same route or track constantly can be boring and I frequently run different ways through my suburban town.

Dogs and cars are the main hazards, however. If you stick to the main roads, dogs don't bother you. But you have to be especially careful of cars. One young member of our New York Road Runners' Club was struck and killed one night while running near Kennedy Airport. And if you are going to run on the side roads, carrying a small stick, a cane or other visible object will usually discourage dogs.

Another precaution—don't run on a full stomach. Wait at least two or three hours after a meal. And, if possible, visit the bathroom before starting the training session. If not, abdominal pain may develop, especially if you are determined to run over 8-10 miles.

Time of training is a matter of personal preference. However, in the hot weather and in periods of high humidity, morning or evening workouts would be better. If you're not used to the heat, running in hot weather can lead to heat exhaustion or heat stroke. Because of the many problems associated with warm weather running, I have tried to get in workouts as close to 1 p.m. as possible in order to become acclimated. When acclimated, your sweat has a very low salt content and you can go long distances without using much water. In fact, I put most of it on my head and also douse myself liberally before starting to run. One has to be careful in a race that the spectators don't get too enthusiastic in pouring water on you. If your shoes and socks get wet, you are a prime candidate for blisters.

Tea and honey is the accepted refreshment along the way, although I have found bouillon to be the best post-race drink, and probably orange slices are of some benefit. As few salt drinks are given along the way, some runners take them before the race. That has not been my practice, but I see no harm in it.

Cold weather requires special clothing. Thermal underwear is excellent. I also put on a pair of painter's gloves and wear a headband to cover my ears. Painter's gloves are inexpensive, but are quite warm and can be discarded in a long race at a trivial cost. Occasionally, in very cold weather I have used a ski mask. Also for very cold or rainy weather I have a light nylon parka which is rain-proof and retains body heat. Some people also use liniment on their legs in cold weather. I have found no particular advantage to that practice.

No matter how careful you are, you are bound to run into some injury. However, I have always maintained that a runner who trains and doesn't strain automatically cuts down on the injury problem. My friend, Tom Osler, a leading eastern distance man, says that all injuries are unnecessary and result from carelessness or fatigue. It is the tired runner who makes a misstep and turns an ankle or gets a bone bruised. Using slow warmups and avoiding speed in workouts usually cancels out muscle pulls, especially of the large thigh muscles, the quadriceps, the hamstrings and even the calf muscles.

When really serious injuries occur, head for the nearest

swimming pool. Although I have had my share of injuries, I have maintained my overall condition by swimming (any style) for an equivalent time, usually 30 minutes, to my running work-out. As I find swimming a bore and not quite the complete exercise, I am glad to get back to the roads.

Another hazard awaits the individual who is serious about his running. Many a runner has had to overcome the psychological roadblock resulting from the reaction of friends, neighbors and even family. However, as soon as they see that your running is not a passing fancy, jokes and jibes stop and you can go your way in peace. But I would urge you to have a private place for your gear. No wife wants her bedroom turned into a locker room.

I f God had meant us to walk, He would have given us feet. And if He'd meant us to play, He would have given us a sport for these ordinary G.I. (God-issued) feet—a sport for rich and poor, for old and young and for either sex; a sport free from injury and interruption; a sport with physical exertion and mental relaxation; a sport that would not penalize ineptitude, but would reward excellence; a sport that is as natural as, for in-stance, walking.

There are a few thousand people who think this describes their sport: race walking. They are part of a ground-swell that may become the wave of the future.

The race walker, for one thing, can make do with ordinary feet. He can put miles and miles and miles on feet that would break down in any other sport. And he isn't likely to get injuries further up in the kinetic chain that goes from foot to leg to knee to thigh to low back. Race walking is virtually injury free.

It is no coincidence that a race walker, not a runner, now holds the record for crossing the United States on foot. Such a venture demands daily pain-free, uninterrupted mileage. And this is where race walking excels.

The main source of this protection is the walker's swivel-hipped form. This prevents bounce and largely cancels out any shock on impact. His foot plant—starting with the heel, riding along the outside of the foot and delivering straight ahead—is just what the Creator planned. And the locked knee, a race walking requirement, keeps the kneecap in its appropriate place, the patellar groove, thus preventing the too-frequent knee problems seen in runners, tennis players and other athletes.

Why this form also wards off sciatica is more difficult to explain. It may be because, as one writer describes walking, "The hips slide into place under the torso, the belly muscles tighten, the spine straightens and toughens." Whatever the reason, sciatica is almost unheard of in race walkers. And some who took up the sport while in the throes of sciatic symptoms have had rapid cures once they started striding through their neighborhoods.

Indeed, race walking is a safe refuge for any injured athlete. It is the perfect sport for recuperating from some other sport. Much like an elderly lady of my acquaintance who was told whatever else was wrong with her would get better while she was having her cataracts out, the ailing athlete who turns to race walking will soon find himself on the mend.

The runner who switches to race walking for this therapeutic effect will discover other assets of the sport that he might not have suspected. A sure way to physical fitness, for instance. Work done by Dr. Michael Pollock at Wake Forest University has shown that it makes little difference on the cardiovascular fitness meter as to whether you run or walk. When intensity, frequency and duration are similar, results are similar.

Race walking, like other sports, takes technique, talent and character. And it has its own rewards. One of these must be in the realm of the mind and the spirit. Race walking has yet to be listed among the ways of reaching a natural high, the ways of altering your consciousness without drugs. But I suspect it is only a matter of time until some race walker mentions this. When he does, he will provide us with answers about other things than race walking.

After all, if God had meant us to understand this world, he would have made us view it at five miles an hour and given us the feet to hold that speed for an eternity.

When some people seek contemplation or conversation, they prefer a seat near a roaring fire on a winter's night. Others choose the seclusion of a sandy dune with the ocean murmuring in the background. Still others desire more commonplace settings. But always the conditions are the same: quiet, beauty, a sense of security and the world immobile.

This may be right for most people, but it's not right for me. What I need is motion. Give me an hour's run and I can rival Aquinas in contemplation and handle the great Sam Johnson in conversation. There on the roads, traffic or not, I have found inexhaustible supplies of two of the rarest commodities in the world today.

One of them, conversation, is rapidly becoming extinct. Man's verbal instinct is to fight or preach. Argument is our forte, not dialogue. If that fails, we go into a sermon. Unfortunately, we find most other kinds of talk difficult. So what passes for dialogue or communication is the verbal ping-pong of the TV talk show, the small talk of the passing-in-corridor variety, or the chatter indulged in at innumerable cocktail parties.

At the least, however, this talking allows the use of the vocal cords and protects them from atrophy. This last is a present danger to the average US household where the TV is on an estimated six hours a day—placing the average American family well on the way to becoming as mute as giraffes.

Running has none of these limitations or hazards. The second wind, which opens the runner to unknown and unsuspected physiological delights, also reveals unexpected insights into his psyche and his inner self. And at the same time, it makes the conversational juices flow.

I have found this state of perspiration and euphoria can perform minor miracles, can eliminate those feelings of guilt which lead to sarcasm and bitterness, can rid me of the righteousness that produces sermons, and can even dispel the self-consciousness that limits me to talk about the weather and the state of my partner's health.

Running frees me from the monosyllabic inanities of my usual tongue-tied state, liberates me from the polysyllabic jargon of my profession, removes me from the kind of talk which aims at concealing rather than revealing what is in my heart and what I mean to do and be.

For me, no time passes faster than when running with a companion. An hour of conversation on the run is one of the quickest and most satisfying hours ever spent. It is rivaled only by those solitary hours when I've been able to withdraw from the world and be inside myself. Such moments can open doors impervious to force or guile.

A midwestern psychiatrist once wrote me about a withdrawn patient who refused to talk to anyone about what was troubling her. It was only when they started to take runs around the institution's grounds that she suddenly began to reveal her basic problems in great detail.

I'm at a loss to know why this happens to runners and those who run with us, but I surmise it has something to do with our deepest instincts about movement. That, at any rate, is the suggestion of Dr. Thomas Harris who wrote the best-seller, *I'm OK—You're OK.*

Harris divides each of us into three parts: Parent (which is life as it is taught by the rule book), Child (which is life as it is felt or wished) and Adult (which is life as we figure it out for ourselves).

The first Adult act we do, says Harris, is locomotion. The Adult in us begins when we take our first step—our first walk to think things over. From then on, we have the recording in our brain that movement is good, that it helps us to see more clearly what our problem is.

Harris is probably right. Walk to clear your mind. Run to clear your mind. If you do, you can see yourself, however imperfect, as a unique adult. When you accept imperfection in yourself, you accept others at face value, too.

My running friends call interval quarter-miles "character-builders." William James, who once described character as completely fashioned will, would have agreed. James saw effort as the thing we are. Strength, intelligence, wealth and good luck are all things we carry. The real question posed to us is what effort we can make.

Interval quarters ask that question. They are the little unnecessary exercises James recommended be done to make it easier for us to "will" what is right. And there are few things more unnecessary than interval quarters. These repetitions done at race pace with brief rest intervals serve no reasonable purpose.

Long slow distance, on the other hand, makes for aerobic fitness, an essential for physical ease and endurance, for general health and even longevity. Further, long slow distance allows moments when body and mind and will fuse in pure joy.

Interval quarters develop anaerobic fitness. They teach the body how to do without oxygen, how to handle lactic acid. This is a worthless skill unless you wish to earn your living running the mile. Only in the final stages do they harmonize the body and mind and will, and then it is a fusion bought with pain and frustration and hard work.

Where distance runs sometimes assure me of a heavenly home, interval quarters remind me that I am dust—a fallen creature who can do so much and no more. And in that, they become important. There may be no better cure for my despair than a 10-mile run, but there is certainly no better antidote to pride than a set of interval quarters.

The first one I find deceptively easy. There is almost no effort in the initial acceleration, the smooth stride down the backstretch, the lean into the turn and then simply holding form through the finish. The breathing quickly returns to normal. The pulse falls to 120. The two-minute wait seems too long.

Again, I'm on the line. Again, the easy first turn and the smooth backstretch. But now the turn is a strain and the finish seems farther away. This two minutes is just enough for breathing and pulse to reach the baseline.

Now the third one. This time I'm looser, my form is better, but the lactic acid is accumulating. Midway in the backstretch, my arms become heavy, my thighs tighten up. I manage to make the turn, but the run to the finish is as bad as an all-out race. Now the two minutes is not enough. I'm breathing 60 times a minute and don't even bother to check the pulse.

Once more I start off. Once more the mysterious ease of the first 10 seconds, but from then on it is a struggle. With a full

220 to go, I feel as bad as I did at the end of the last one. My chest is rebelling at the impossible task of supplying air. The pain increases as I breathe faster and faster without catching up.

Somehow, I hold form. The heavy, cumbersome, slowly responding legs somehow manage a lift through the final yards. But now I am on my hands and knees, the stopwatch ticking away. I'm like a fighter taking his full nine count before getting off the canvas.

I get up with seconds to go and accept the final test. Within 50 yards, I begin to come apart. Lactic acid is engulfing me. The body has had enough, the will is ready to capitulate, the mind is seeking sanity. Somehow, I have to bring what is impossible and unnecessary and irrational into one "yes"—one affirmation that will carry me through to the end.

The only way I can succeed is by staking my whole self on the outcome. If I am to enjoy freedom and ecstasy and fulfillment running on a country road, I must accept discipline and responsibility and commitment on a quarter-mile track. For those moments, the answer to the question "Who am I?" is in the pure and unnecessary effort of that final lap.

I turned to teaching," a college professor told a friend of mine, "for three reasons: June, July and August." He was thinking of summer at Cape Cod—the sort of summer described by psychiatrist-author Robert Jay Lifton: "with the incomparable dunes and the magnificent ocean; the rhythm of the days and nights—the unparalleled purity of work and play devoid of interuptions, irrelevancies and necessities."

A person could turn to running for those three reasons. June, July and August give you running at its best. Here also are those incomparable dunes and the magnificent ocean. The runner too can find the rhythm of the days and nights. And no one better can divest himself of interruptions, irrelevancies and necessities.

For him, the summer changes with the time of day. There is morning with the bright coolness of the new day and the smell of fresh cut grass. Or afternoon filled with a close, heavy heat and sweat dripping from elbow to wrist and salty in the eyes and mouth. And the soft warm evenings on a run to the beach and the first chilling plunge into the surf and the long floating wait under the surface feeling your body seal-like in the water.

And then there are the races. Monday evenings at Takanassee, the sun still in the west but more light than burning. Evenings perfect for an unhurried lazy hour of talking and getting your number and stretching and gentle ribbing and warming up. Then a cruel 20 minutes and a pleasant exhaustion. Evenings ending at the surfers' beach and another swim more ritual than wanted.

And other races. The painful 10-milers. Westport, for instance. Battling distance and hills and heat and humidity. But no nectar the Greeks ever imagined could come up to a cold soda at the finish line at Westport.

So summer is the ultimate sensual experience in this basic human activity. Heat and humidity call upon the limits of human physiology. The runner in summer comes to know the human animal.

For that animal, June, July and August are white sand and green grass and blue ocean. For him, summer is shade and sun, the heaviness at noon and the cooling southeaster at four. But most of all it is water. Water taken in, water sweated out, water jumped into, water thrown on you. It is rain water and sweat water and sea water. It is Coke and Gatorade and orange juice. It is cold showers and ice at the nape of your neck. It is dew in the morning and afternoon showers. In short, summer is an elemental primeval experience to the runner.

But now this season is over. The days are growing short. It is now dark before supper is done. Summer has gone. And with it the summer runs, the races, the expanded 24-hour cycle of light and dark, of days and nights. You might say the year is over—over for the college professor and the runner.

Or is it just the beginning? There are three other reasons for being a runner. September, October and November. Already there is a nip in the morning air. Soon the leaves will start to turn. Cross-country is just around the corner. Cross-country. Its name hurls defiance to city and suburbs. Over the river and through the woods, says cross-country.

The lushness of summer is gone, the senses grow sharper.

Autumn is all feeling and smelling. The crisp days. The cool nights. Now once more you need a warmup and a sweat suit. These are the best days for training. Forty-five to 50 degrees makes the body go best. And races everywhere every week. The runner knows again the sights and sounds and smells of Van Cortlandt and Warinanco, of Fairmount and Central Park. Autumn is no time to leave.

And what of December, January and February? Winter is a season of contrasts. Long runs in frigid weather and five-hour car trips for a five-minute race in a smoke-filled gym. Winter is all adrenalin and starters' guns, bone-chilling afternoon runs and nights with afghans, quilts and comforters. The hot shower is back. Winter is a season no one would miss.

But if you stopped, it couldn't be in springtime. March, April and May put it all together, the marathon and the mile. Boston and the Penn Relays back to back. Exhaustion two ways, the one aerobic and legs gone, the other anaerobic and the chest in agony. Spring is getting dressed in front of a TV camera in the Hopkinton Gym and in front of a girl sprinter having a thigh pull massaged in a Franklin Field dressing room. Spring is running with a thousand people at Boston and 10 in Philadephia. Spring is wonderful and you must be there.

Four

Runners and Walkers

I am a runner. Years back, that statement would have meant little more to me than an accidental choice of sport—a leisure-time activity selected for reasons as superficial as the activity itself.

Now I know better. The runner does not run because he is too slight for football or hasn't the ability to put a ball through a hoop or can't hit a curveball. He doesn't run primarily to lose weight or become fit or to prevent heart attacks. He runs because he has to. In being a runner, in moving through pain and fatigue, in imposing stress upon stress, in eliminating all but the necessities of life, he is fulfilling himself and becoming the person he is.

I have given up many things in this "becoming" process. None was a sacrifice. When something clearly became non-essential, there was no problem in doing without. And when something clearly became essential, there was no problem accepting it and whatever went with it.

Whatever I gave up—whatever innocent indulgences, ordinary pleasures or extraordinary vices—I gave up from some inner compulsion, not in a mood of self-sacrifice or from a sense of duty. I was simply doing what came naturally.

For the runner, less is better. The life that is his work of art is understated. His needs are little, his wants few: one friend, few clothes, a meal now and then, some change in his pockets, and for enjoyment his thoughts and the elements.

I see this simplicity as my perfection. In the eyes of observers, however, it appears completely different. My success in removing myself from things and people, from ordinary ambition and desires, is seen as lack of caring, proof of uninvolvement and failure to contribute.

So be it. A larger view of the world might include the possibility that such people are necessary. The runner who is burning with a tiny flame on some lonely road does somehow contribute. A world composed solely of runners might be unworkable, but a world without them would be unliveable.

When seen from car or bus or train, the pedestrian awalk or ajog seems much the same. Except for attire and speed, the walker and runner seem to be brothers under the skin—solitary and cerebral rebels in silent and meditative protest against our modern ways.

And, in part, this is true. Both walker and runner have found fulfillment in pursuits this jet-age world finds ludicrous. In an affluent society, we must have affluent leisure-time activities. If we are being paid in multiples of $5 an hour, our leisure time should be worth that and more. If we have invested in cars and boats and stereos and other marvels of leisure technology, our recreation must be spent with these expensive toys.

Paradoxically, the more time we have off, the less time we have to ourselves. Time and space are the new luxuries. And avocations like walking and running—which occupy so much time and demand so much open space—are too slow and costly for our high-priced leisure economy.

The runner and walker alone seem to find satisfaction in this slow transport of the human body across the countryside. Their delight with a pace of 3-10 miles an hour must be considered atavistic in times when cars cruise at 70 and planes at 600.

But despite these common joys, the runner and walker are entirely different persons. The runner is still concerned with the conquering of space and time. He logs miles the way lesser men build their savings accounts. He has 50-mile weeks and 100-mile weeks and 150-mile weeks. He runs with a goal and a purpose, training himself with gradually increasing loads, preparing himself for the ultimate effort, trying to reach his own perfection.

All of this calls for constant attention—attention to breathing, to arm movement, to the rhythm of the thighs, to the acceleration of the straightened leg. These details must continually occupy him, for only through this unnatural awareness can he attain the classical yet instinctual form of the champion.

The walker is past all this. For him, observation and thought dominate. His qualifications, according to Emerson, include vast curiosity, good speed, good silence and an eye for nature. Like Hawthorne, the walker looks for enough to feed the human spirit for a single day. Like Hawthorne, he is a peaceful outlaw "plunging into a cool bath of solitude."

If this suggests that walkers are mature men with a capacity for observation, men with empathy for their environment, it is because it always has been so. Walkers have been the philosophers, the thinkers, the artists of their age. The Greeks had their peripatetic (walk-around) school of philosophy set up by Aristotle. And Demosthenes was said to have perfected his elocution while walking the beach. The most ardent of more recent walkers was the poet Wordsworth, who was said to have logged 175,000 miles during his daily 3-4-hour jaunts. This is a mark possibly equaled by Thoreau but few others.

It was Thoreau who wrote, "I think I cannot preserve my health or spirits unless I spend four hours a day sauntering through the woods and over the hills and fields."

Health and fitness, then, are part of the values of walking. But for intellectual creativity and enjoyment, walking is unsurpassed. "In walking," wrote Oliver Wendell Holmes, "the will and the muscles are so accustomed to working together and perform their task with so little expenditure of force that the intellect is left comparatively free."

Where all other athletes must be in attention to the way they move, the walker can retire into a reverie of complete detachment. The walker can find his inner world (and outer world, too) no more than a short stroll from home. He steps out his front door, views the universe and knows it is good. The walker has found the peace that the runner still seeks.

While on a mid-morning run, I had a narrow escape from serious injury. A driver coming up behind me saw me in his path at the last possible second, and by maximum use of his brakes stopped in time. The reaction of a group of teenagers closeby was hilarity. They found this near-catastrophe highly amusing.

I wasn't surprised. The runner knows of man's inhumanity to man first-hand. Taunts, bottles and other objects are thrown at him from passing cars. Some drivers deliberately backfire as they go by, or even try to run him down. A few runners have actually been set upon and beaten up.

Why is this? Why is the runner a lightning rod for the anger and aggression and violence of others? Why does this hapless, vulnerable non-combatant bring out these qualities in his fellow men?

Precisely because the runner is nobody's fellow man, and his fellow men know it. There is a metaphysical lawlessness about running. The runner puts himself above law, above society. He is a law unto himself. And men in gangs and crowds and mobs know this and react accordingly.

The runner follows no one's law but his own. He cares for little but the workings of his own mind and body. He would, as one runner told me, rather give up his best friend than give up running. He cares even less for the institutions that protect and support him. He despises authority and, if anything, agrees with Auguste Compte, who wrote that participation in government is fundamentally degrading.

He further alienates those who see the crowd as carnival where everyone joins in, becoming one happy, amorphous glob. The runner is an ascetic. Pleasure is painful to him. Singing and dancing and even talking to another human being are avoided at all costs.

When he runs on the roads, he is making a comment about life. He is, in effect, criticizing the life-style of everyone who

sees him. He may not want to do this, but he does. He is putting down those who smoke and drink and socialize and call everyone by their first name. He has given up on that world and those in it, and has gone inside himself. No wonder those who live by the rules, or live by community, feel threatened by him.

Seen this way, what happens to runners is the just wrath of a society pushed too far. Those who believe we should all be one, as citizens or brothers, see the runner as a loner who never will contribute to the common good. That, they say, is man's real inhumanity to man. And they may be right. In this world, no one is innocent.

What Jim Bouton's *Ball Four* did for baseball and Dave Meggysey's *Out of Their League* did for football, Hal Higdon's *On the Run from Dogs and People* has done for long distance running.

Not that Higdon has a best-seller on his hands. Distance running is not a spectator sport, which limits his audience. Besides, he has not spiced it up with revelations about drugs and sex, and the only four-letter word which recurs with any frequency is "pain."

But he has accomplished what he set out to do. He has explained these healthy, happy, somewhat remote and more than a little peculiar runners to themselves and their fellow citizens.

This explanation is made easier because Higdon is himself the prototype distance runner. Which is to say that he has made steady progress since his college days as a lean, hungry and mediocre miler to his present status as a lean, hungry and mediocre marathoner (although he did once finish fifth at Boston).

He also went through the necessary conversion from dilettante to true believer, but only after he had sunk, so to speak, to the gutter—stopping after 14 miles in his first Boston

"At the age of 26," he writes, "I found I was a quitter." Route 9 from Hopkinton to Boston became his Road to Damascus. There the dilettante died and the true believer, the fanatic, the free man, was born.

Now in his 40s and the distance runners' author-in-residence, Higdon tells in his and their own words what manner of men they are and why they act the way they do. Characteristically, he belittles the importance of running in his introduction. He leads a balanced life, he says.

"Running occupies but one hour of the day. Many people spend that much time working on crossword puzzles." But no one is likely to accept the sophistry that running is simply an incidental part of Higdon's Good Life. By the same standard, Sir Lawrence Olivier spends only an hour or so a day in the theatre.

This explanation won't wash, and Higdon doesn't really expect us to believe it. It is normal for the runner to be subtle. He hates the obvious, or to be obvious, which is one of the reasons running on the road in sight of his neighbors bothers him.

What should be obvious is the philosophy of these introverts: "I run, therefore I am." And that, explicit or not, is the message of Higdon's book. The distance runner, he tells us, is using his sport to survive in a hostile, competitive world he didn't make and is not made for him.

It also is apparent on these pages that this survival means growth, and the peculiar phenomenon of growth with age. Age, it seems, holds no terrors for these thin, bony people with their alert, bird-like faces. For them, youth has no special charm.

What these cadaveric specimens dread are such things as forcible socializing (they adjust to stress by withdrawal), encounters with dogs (they make bad initial impressions, especially with animals) or police (they usually have had inferior feelings before authority figures since childhood), and aggression (they are hypersensitive to pain, both psychic and physical, and would rather run themselves to oblivion than be punched in the nose).

Where, then, is happiness for these late-maturing running machines?

The backbone of the runner's day and life is that daily workout—Higdon's "only one hour." Some run marathons because, as one runner stated, "I forget how terrible the last one was." But everyone runs workouts because they remember how pleasant or exhilarating or relaxing or rewarding the last one was.

This is why runners find contemplation, identity and a degree of happiness in those long, solitary hours on the road.

Unfortunately, they have a genius for being misunderstood and rarely express these thoughts except under pressure.

Higdon tells of one such incident. An Ohio runner got some icy stares while passing a congregation leaving a church service one Sunday morning. He finally said to one church-goer, "Look, I've seen more of God in the last seven miles than you'll see in that church the rest of your days."

The introduction to the Mass of the Runner," said the Jesuit seated at the living room window overlooking the ocean and the dunes, "will be from a passage by Amby Burfoot."

The distance runners of every age strewn on chairs and stairs and floor gave a sigh of assent. They conjured up the figure of the stork-like Burfoot as he won the Boston marathon in 1968.

"I run," the non-running Jesuit read, "because I enjoy it— not always, but most of the time. I run because I've always run— not trained, but run."

Beyond the priest in slacks and sweater, the runners could see the narrow boardwalk where they had run five miles to start the celebration.

"What do I get?" The words of Burfoot, a Connecticut Yankee, came in the Boston accent of the priest. "Joy and pain. Good health and injuries. Exhilaration and despair. A feeling of accomplishment and a feeling of waste. The sunrise and the sunset."

The first hymn followed. It was James Taylor's "On a Country Road." The young knew the words. The elders knew the feeling. The congregation of loners were beginning to come together. Showered and content after the run and a festive meal meal of hamburgers and Coke, they were bound by one tie: running.

Tell me a man is a runner, I thought, and I know more about him than if you said he was a Christian. Say he is a football player and I know more about his creed than if you told me he was an agnostic. Tell me he plays the horses and it says more than the fact that he's an American.

Why do people run? The pain, the pleasure, the sunrise, the sunset, said the Jesuit, are enough to answer why we do anything. Love, marry, work, bear children, raise families.

"Is running," he asked, "merely a symbol?"

The runners attempted to answer. "I ran away from things all my life before I started running," said one. "Now I'm happy and I don't know exactly why." Another, presently injured, said he had been unable to replace running in his daily life. Others saw themselves as different, more complete. One looked to the day of no more competition, when there would be no winning or losing, just running and the enjoyment of it.

The priest blessed the bread and wine. There was silence and a rush of feeling.

The Mass was ending, and the runners rose to greet each other. Men, it is said, live together and die alone. Runners live alone and die or suffer together. Only after a race does their reserve dissolve. In that common agony, they can reveal themselves to each other.

"We are completely happy," said someone near me, "doing something that would drive other people crazy." And vice versa, it seems.

"Go in peace," said the Jesuit. And we did. We truly did.

Five

Racing and Chasing

The race is the beauty part. Practice is fun, and laughs, and even tough with those interval halves. And there are those days when you don't even know you are running, like when you drive to work and don't remember passing familiar places along the way. Practice can soothe you or exhaust you, but it's never the same as the race.

The time you put it all together is the race. For one thing, there's the anxiety, the apprehension that must be minimized but not avoided. Or else you come to the starting line completely flat. But you can get too much of that peculiar empty feeling —the tightness in the stomach, the urge to yawn. The answer is enough adrenalin but not too much.

Next comes the warmup. An easy six minutes and the sweating starts. You search for indications. Will the day be good or bad? The warmup tells nothing.

On the starting line for that one silent moment. Then the start. Always faster than you remembered. The mind goes through the instructions. Relax. Push off with each stride. Run from the hips. Belly breathe.

At the half-mile mark, you settle for a pace that keeps breathing just bearable. Everything makes a difference. Every change in footing—grass, cinder, dirt or stone. A grade that would escape a surveyor adds its toll. The environment occupies you completely. Wind speed and direction, temperature and humidity can either aid or hinder. Forget the watch; the course runs different every time.

A mile past and the first hill. Quite suddenly every step is an exquisite effort. The slope steepens and each foot takes its interminable time. The top comes and there is relief to burning chest and aching legs. Now they come in series. Toil up and fly down. Then out onto the flats for the three-mile mark. There are the stop watches and your friends—an occasional face sharply seen. The hearing is keener than the eye. "They're dead up ahead. Get tough."

You're alone again, remembering now is the time to make your move. Relax, the race is in front of you. So you push off. Run with your thighs. Use that trailing leg. And now comes Cemetery Hill with its easy winding approach. And then 100 yards straight up. The legs are gone, the breathing impossible. Your face is at your knees. Your thoughts turn to survival. But finally there is the crest. But not before an additional rise not seen from below. The incredible oxygen debt is finally paid off in a halting downhill stagger.

The flats once more. The finish in sight but you are beginning to come apart. Pain is now your companion. It warns you to a point that must not be passed. So you wait and endure until the moment for the final drive to the finish. Now! Now there is no tomorrow. The world and time have narrowed to this agony. Where the legs hurt, you hurt them more. But the chest can't be helped. The light is starting to go out. And then you're over the line.

Ten minutes later, you wonder why you didn't push harder going up Cemetery Hill.

I traveled the whole world looking for adventure, and found it in my own body," a writer friend of mine told me shortly after completing his first race. He is not one to use words lightly. His adventure is the true adventure.

My friend had made the leap from running to racing, from

play to sport, from child to man. His training runs had prepared him for the challenge, but they were not the challenge. Those runs were pure play. They had no start, no finish. They had no rules, no officials. They began and ended by whim or boredom or pleasure.

The race was sport. It had a start, a finish, rules and officials. It began and existed through the will and commitment of the athletes. It was life in a bounded situation, filled with effort and risk, uncertainty and tension. Here, a decision to quit—of little moment in a practice session—could become a statement of yourself, your character.

My friend finished far back in the race. No matter. The race allows for this. The struggle that the Greeks called "agon" (from which comes our "agony") is there for winner and loser alike—as are those briefly splendid moments that accompany them when we realize our finest potential.

Only the race allows for this. The runs may be meditation and all that implies. But the race is experience—the transformation of you or me meditating to you or me as we are, to knowing who we actually are and what we actually can do.

The training runs may put us in touch with the source of our inspiration, our creativity and our intuitive flashes of understanding. But the race is reality. Here, we are stripped. Here, even name, rank and serial number are irrelevant. In this seemingly artificial situation, we put ourselves to the practical test.

The race allows us to push ourselves to the absolute limit, to share however briefly and symbolically in the tragedy all around us. And more than that, in this advent, this new birth, I not only become a man but accept the man I am.

The race is one place where two contradictory ideas about life can exist. The first is that everything done well is inherently a criticism of anything done poorly; the second, if a thing is worth doing it is worth doing badly. In a marathon, the winner's perfect race is a criticism of anything less well done. Yet a middle-aged runner who finishes two hours later can sit and cry with happiness.

Defeat, then, can be as revealing as victory and seen for

what it is—a learning experience. If we are to invent a plot for our existence, we must know exactly who we are. Untried, unchallenged, we would never know. And we know in our bones that the poet Robinson Jeffers was right when he said, "In pleasant ease and security, how soon the soul of man begins to die."

I ran a mile for Roger Bannister. I relived the 3:59.4 Bannister ran at the Iffley Road track in Oxford 20 years earlier. I ran a mile for all milers, for all those who have accepted the challenge of the perfect distance and have sought to run that perfect race.

I didn't want to run it. I wasn't ready to run it. And the mile is not to be entered lightly. When Bannister was to race one, he looked according to his friends like a man going to the electric chair.

"Few understand," Bannister wrote, "the mental agony through which an athlete must pass before he can give his maximum—and how rarely, if he is built such as I, he can give it."

But this was a special day, and something special had to be done. My stomach had that all-gone feeling, and when I thought of the race my chest would tighten with anxiety.

Why this worry? Why be nervous when other distances are a lark? I'm not sure, but all milers know this feeling. For one thing, the mile is the true measure of a runner. It demands a unique mixture of your maximum speed, strength and endurance, while in other races any one of these will do. And it is the classic confrontation with the stopwatch, where moments no more than a pause in a conversation damn you as a runner and a man.

If you come to a mile with less than your own perfection, the mile will search it out. The mile is a lonely and painful and beautiful place. And it must be run, as the poetess wrote of love, "to the depth and breadth and height my soul can reach."

So this is no ordinary race that can be run again and again. Milers run few miles in competition and none in practice. The mile is the culmination of months of training, the final accomplishment of the athlete's year. That year starts in September with long runs over the autumn countryside, and continues through a winter of further extending the body's endurance, and then finally a spring of quarter-miles that would test a saint.

These quarters are voluntary acts of torture with two short minutes in between that leave me on hands and knees, my breath coming in gasps, my groans audible to bewildered spectators. And the thought goes through my head that I never want to feel this way again.

But these quarters teach the mind and will to accept pain. They teach the body to provide energy without the use of oxygen. They teach it to convert lactic acid and delay an inevitable collapse. Bannister worked this out. He formulated the training and convinced himself it could be done. He put his life into this one-mile race. And by April of 1954, he was running 10 consecutive quarters in 59 seconds.

I came to my mile 20 years later without those interval quarters, without the preparation the mile deserves, and without those companions Bannister had—Brasher to pace him that first half and Chataway the third quarter. I wasn't ready for the race, but I gave it the respect due it.

We set out together, myself and five freshmen who looked like my acolytes, lifting easily through that first quarter in 74 seconds. ("I slipped in behind Brasher," reported Bannister, "feeling tremendously full of running.") We reached the half in 2:32, a respectable pace for 14-year-olds and anyone in his 50s.

But then the altar boys disappeared in my wake, and I was left with the tightening legs and burning chest and the taste in my mouth that I get when I am running faster and longer than I actually can. So I came to the end of the three-quarters already eight seconds over my 5:00 pace and with nothing left. ("at the end of three-quarters," Bannister stated, "the effort was still barely perceptible.")

But because the mile is what it is and milers are what they are, I ran that last quarter as perfectly as I could. I staggered here and there, the body protesting that the whole thing was ridiculous, but the mind and will somewhere safe from pain demanding I do more and more. ("In the last 50 yards," Bannister revealed, "my body had long since exhausted its energy but it went on running just the same.")

Then it was over and I was kneeling, feeling the soft earth, the sun warming me, the grass friendly in my hands.

"If I faltered," wrote Bannister, "there would be no arms to hold me and the world would be a cold and forbidding place." But he had not, nor had I, and on this day the world had its arms open wide, and it was a soft and warm and friendly and wonderful place.

What makes the Boston marathon great? Is it, perhaps, April? The Boston has pre-empted April, leaving other and lesser months to other and lesser marathons. It has taken the April of Chaucer's gentle showers, when people "long to go on pilgrimages." It has seized the April of T. S. Eliot: "The cruelest month breeding/Lilacs out of the dead land mixing/Memory and desire."

The poets tell it all. Scatter-brained April, so unpredictable but still our best hope. Behind lies the long, hard and possibly futile winter. Ahead, a perfect day and a perfect marathon?

What makes the Boston marathon great? Part of the answer is April. The rest, if the runner in me is right, is the course. Runners have spent their lifetimes observing, analyzing, dissecting and running marathons. They should know what makes a great marathon course. They have made Boston "the mother of marathons."

Wind, heat and humidity add to the natural contours, which make the course a continually changing challenge. Boston has that quality of real greatness. It is a course that may be beaten but never defeated. Challenge the Boston and you must be at your peak. Accept your limitations and, with care, the thinking runner will have a comfortable, creditable race. But go for broke and prepare to be broken.

The key to all of this is the hills. They are an ever-present consideration. The first slope is downhill. It comes immediately, stretches for over a mile and lures both veteran and tyro into an abnormally fast pace. Even should one recognize the danger to his pace, he is powerless to prevent the attrition on his previously unused (in practice) checking muscles as downhill follows downhill during the first two-thirds of the race.

But these are merely banderillas. The death blow, if it is to be struck, comes at the 20-mile mark—Heartbreak Hill. Heartbreak is fourth and longest and steepest of a series of long, steep grades which begin at 17 miles. Heartbreak is not only fearsome in itself, but it comes at the very moment when the body reaches the physiological (and probably psychological) make-or-break point. Here is, if it is anywhere, the moment of truth.

Tragedy, which is man wanting to be more than he is and failing at it, is upon you, and Heartbreak magnifies it to heroic proportions. April is indeed the cruelest month.

But if hills can be your downfall, cannot hills be your salvation?

Hills do many things for a runner. They force him into the most economical style, a great asset for the distances. They strengthen the muscles needed for the assault on these obstacles in a race. And they allow him the grandeur and euphoria of that finest hour when he goes floating through the Newton Hills and then takes the last downhill at Boston College, entering Boston full of run.

The day may come when all that will be past—when marathons are uniform and we have a Tartan track, absolutely level and extending 13 miles 192½ yards out and then back. The statisticians who like their records neat and tidy and without asterisks will take over.

Until then we all have Boston and April, and a race worth a lifetime of running.

I learned how much the body can stand," said Dr. Fred Blanton, a 40-year-old Florida ophthalmologist, after running the Boston marathon. "You don't know what pain is until you get up around 21 or 22 miles. You just hurt like hell. You'd give anything in the world to quit, but you just keep going. The people who run these all the time must be masochists."

Others, besides Blanton, have taken this position. Olympian

George Young, who qualified for the Mexico City marathon as insurance for making the team, experienced the same pain. When asked later whether he expected to better his time when he ran the marathon again, he answered, "Anyone who would run more than one of these is nuts."

Why would anyone run more than one? It's a good question, especially if the marathon is in Atlantic City. In weather, crowds, course and coverage, the Atlantic City/Road Runners Club marathon is strictly Class D compared to Boston. At Atlantic City, the competitors outnumber the crowd. The temperature is usually out of good running range and the humidity excessive. But the course is the main hazard.

To the first-timer at Atlantic City, it appears to be the place to run your personal best marathon. I doubt if there is a grade of more than one foot on the entire route. You go out and back three times—which gives you three chances to stop right where the sweatsuits and blankets and hot showers are. On an out-and-back course, when you hit the turn at a little over 13 miles you feel at least relieved that you're heading home. And at Boston every step is taking you closer to the finish. But leaving friends and warmth and comfort at the 17-mile mark and starting out again is often more than a non-masochist can stand.

Atlantic City may look easy, but it never is. Those who came to break three hours, or 3½, or four all find that leveling the course is no panacea. The pain and agony are built into the 26 miles, not the terrain.

This pain and agony is sometimes expected and accepted. Ron Hill says, "The fear of running a long race can come from the fact that you know it's going to be physically painful. And unless you are a masochist, nobody likes pain. And if you dwell on this, it can make you nervous." According to Hill, he can talk about where the pain is going to come and how distressing it's going to be without actually "thinking that it's the guy who's speaking who will be in that position."

But it also is a pain that is sometimes forgotten, like the pains of childbirth. So a runner moving surely and confidently

in those final miles reaches that 21-mile mark and suddenly the pain is there. And for the first time he remembers how terrible it was the last time, and how terrible it's going to be now and in the forever that is this race.

Sooner or later, he will think about running the marathon again. Not, perhaps, slumped in the locker room, or on his hands and knees taking a shower, or even on the long painful ride home, but sooner or later. The perfect marathon is like the perfect wave, and every marathoner keeps looking for it. On that day, he will run his best pace all the way, and when he comes to the 21-mile mark he will feel as if he just started and what he has gone through was just a warmup. Then he will float through those last six miles, strong and full of running. And even when he finishes he will feel like running and running and running.

What makes cowards of us all is not conscience as Shakespeare suggested, not fatigue as Vince Lombardi claimed, but pain. Pain and fear of that pain is our undoing. Nowhere is this more evident than in athletics.

For the trained athlete, pain is his major enemy. Already disciplined to the long training schedule, the curtailment of social life and the separation from other interests, the athlete even at the top of his powers still must endure pain beyond his imagination and capacity if he wishes to get maximal performance.

"Your stomach feels as though it's going to fall out," writes Don Schollander, "every kick hurts like hell—and suddenly you hear a shrill internal scream. Then you have a choice. Most swimmers back away. If you push through the pain barrier into real agony, you're a champion."

Runners have told of the same tortures. The muscles gradually hardening up into painful leaden stumps. The breath shortening to convulsive gasps. The chest filled with dry fire. The stomach threatening to explode in agony.

And again the difference between athletes is the peculiar ability—Roger Bannister describes it as a capacity for mental excitement—which enables the runner to ignore or overcome discomfort and pain.

"It is this psychological factor—beyond the ken of physiology—which sets the razor's edge between victory and defeat," Bannister says, "and which determines how closely an athlete comes to the absolute limits of performance."

The barrier that pain puts up to the absolute limits was known as far back as the days of William James. "Beyond the very extremity of fatigue and distress," James wrote, "we may find amounts of ease and power we never dreamed ourselves to own, sources of strength never taxed at all because we never push through the obstruction."

Being a physical coward of long standing (I was once sent home from a dentist's waiting room never having gotten into his chair) the expectation of pain is, alone, enough to unsettle me. I am living testimony to Mary Baker Eddy's claim that "disease is fear made manifest in the body." And all I had for encouragement for those final suffering seconds of a race was the alarming advice of two great coaches, the late Pete Waters and the irrepressible Percy Cerutty.

"Any race you can walk away from," Waters used to say, "is a bad race."

And before I passed out, I could remember Cerutty's words: "If it hurts, make it hurt more."

Help for this coward came from an unexpected source. Grantly Dick Read. Read probably doesn't know who Cerutty is, or even that 50-and-over people run races. Pregnant women are his specialty and natural childbirth is his game. *Childbirth Without Fear* is the Read text—and I was going to change that to *Racing Without Fear*. Surely only labor and delivery among daily experiences could come up to the pain I was enduring in the last quarter of a race. And only that among life's common experiences exposes us to the same fear and apprehension. Grantly Dick Read, the man who made childbirth a conscious joyful act, was about to make his debut in athletics.

So here I was on the line—looking forward with joy and happiness instead of dread and apprehension. The race would not only be painless, I told myself, it would be a wonderful human experience. (Suggestion and autohypnosis, according to some painless labor advocates, can raise resistance to fatigue by more than 20%.)

Oddly enough, it *was* a wonderful experience. The first three-quarters was beautiful. Down the backstretch I started to get the signals in the chest, the legs and the stomach. But now I knew. These were not pains; they are the feelings of any body when it is functioning at its best. Into the last turn, and now what in the past was pain was a warm spreading feeling something like a hot shower after a workout.

The last hundred yards was the best. I was past pain. I won driving and in another world. For which I thank Grantly Dick Read.

There is no man," writes Loren Eiseley, "there are only men."
Each of us lives a life unpredictable by any other—and unfortunately as concealed from its owner as it is from the observer. We are constantly trying to find what our life is and how to live it. This discovery entails taking risks, accepting challenges, going to the very edge of our capabilities. There is no other way. We can pick the time and the stakes, but we must find our game and play it.

My game is the marathon. For me, this is the supreme challenge. In this race, I reach the absolute edge of what my mind and heart and body can do. It is to me what the sheer face of a cliff is to a mountain climber, what white water is to a canoeist.

My risk seems nothing compared to those faced at high altitudes or on raging rivers. People are dying in those places, more than a few because of James Dickey's novel (and movie) *Deliverance*, which popularized this kind of risk-taking.

Dickey is an advocate of the if-your-life-bores-you, risk-it school. What most of us need, he thinks, is a full shot of adrenalin brought on by the proximity of danger. "Then everything," he says, "takes on enormous significance."

For Dickey, adrenalin is an addictive drug, but benign and life-restoring rather than destructive. It restores, he claims, a sense of consequence to what we do. Given the temper of the times, the lack of challenges, the absence of risk, it is no wonder people are trying themselves out in white water and dying in the attempt.

Dickey deplores this. Foolhardiness has no place in any adult search for yourself. It will not help you find the edge between yourself and self-destruction. To arrive at that place, you have to have preparation in strength and speed and endurance. You have to know what to do and when to do it. You must come to the test a whole man.

After the test comes that marvelous calm that follows completing a marathon or climbing a mountain or running the rapids. And with that calm comes the real reward—"the gentle, sentimental things you can do," Dickey tells us, "because of the extraordinarily brutal and painful things you have endured undergoing the risk."

In that calm, I become the man I would like to be—and perhaps I am.

Six

Before and After

My war with the garment industry began when I was 11. I was a city boy newly arrived at the seashore, and the boy next door invited me sailing. It was a first for me and also, unfortunately, for my mother. She dressed me in a regular suit with short pants, added a shirt and topped it off with a tie arranged in a bow and a Buster Brown collar. Not since H.M.S. Pinafore has a sailor been attired in such a costume.

That outing had considerable impact on my clothes from then on. I became a card-carrying member of the fashion conspiracy. I wore whatever was popular. I capitulated to pork-pie hats, pleated trousers and padded shoulders. In time, I accepted cordovan shoes and grey flannel suits, buttoned-down collars and madras ties. I dressed the way everyone else dressed. The important thing about clothes was not to get separated from the herd. Their function was to give you cover, to confer anonymity.

Then I began running and everything changed. For the first time, I saw that clothes had a function. In fact, they had many functions. I discovered that the way I dressed could help my running, could protect me from cold and retain body heat, could improve my circulation and maintain my blood pressure.

Appearance ceased to be a factor. Physiology, not fashion, became the dominant theme of my apparel. And as it became functional, as it began to fill its purpose, my running gear developed a style of its own.

Since it was winter when I started, the basic element of this style was the long-john underwear. The simplicity and elegance of this staple of clothing was lost on my family. There was much talk at home aimed at restricting me to the backyard, where I would be visible to only a few of the more understanding neighbors. There was also the hope that I would move on to more orthodox and presumably more attractive warmup outfits.

That never did happen. Long-johns act as a second skin. They prevent heat loss from the large femoral arteries that course down the inner thighs, and they give a pleasantly discernible support to the legs and lower abdomen. This pressure applied from ankles to navel gives me the equivalent of the astronauts' "G" suit which keeps the force of gravity from interfering with the normal flow of circulating blood.

Where the skin is tight, you need tight clothing. But higher, where the skin is loose to allow for breathing and motion, you need loose clothing. Here, I found a large-sized cotton turtle-neck shirt with long sleeves to be ideal. The sleeves can be varied in position according to the temperature, something not possible with buttoned cuffs. And the turtle-neck collar controls heat loss from the two large carotid arteries that traverse the exposed area from collar bone to the angle of the jaw.

Just as I use my clothing to maintain my physiological equilibrium, I use it to maintain my psychological equilibrium. I sometimes dress in energetic red, sometimes in cheerful yellow. You may see me moving through the countryside in my calm, contented blue or a happy, optimistic orange. Rarely will you see me in black.

I will never buy another suit or shirt or tie or a pair of dress shoes. I have translated my running experience into everyday dress. I now wear skin-tight Levis, over-the-calf hose, some old running shoes and a cotton turtle-neck shirt. When the weather demands, I add a light wool sweater and a nylon windbreaker.

Anything added to this is simply for concealment, a camouflage to keep this second skin and its various colors from public view. For this reason, the ideal warmup suit is a gray nondescript Salvation Army reject which is warm and has pockets to hold keys and glasses and entry fees. Thus attired, I can get to the starting line without arousing comment. I can also be sure that when I finish it will still be there. No one would bother to steal it.

In sport, as in anything else, those who have, get. Those in the money sports go first class.

Lying back now, I can see myself in a pro football locker room—bright, warm and carpeted with soft music piped in and the TV team setting up a commercial for a new hair oil or antiperspirant. I am seated in front of my locker deciding which of my 16 pairs of shoes to wear in today's game. Down the aisle are showers with nozzles as big as those in the old Hotel Astor, and taking a shower is like being wiped out at Redondo Beach.

From the other direction comes the wonderful aroma of liniment radiating from the trainers and their marvelous ministrations, the taping and the massages and the slapping of those suddenly supple muscles. In the corner, someone is icing the post-game Coke and beer.

But then I come back to reality. I'm a runner, not a football player. He goes first-class, I go steerage. So I run out of a Volkswagen. My car is my dressing room. And although it is bright and warm and carpeted and has music piped in, from there on nothing that happens to me bears any resemblance to a day in the life of a pro.

My reality is that some meets have no showers, some meets have no toilet facilities and some meets don't even have a place to dress. But life being what it is and runners what they are, I grab the entry money and the highway tolls and set out to win what passes for fame and fortune in the running game.

This is the main reason you can find me almost any Sunday changing into my running gear in the front seat of my VW. It is an area not quite as roomy as those Wilt Chamberlain commercials would have you believe. And it seems even smaller at the critical point midway in this procedure, especially when I suddenly realize there are some strollers closing in on me. Such happenings make any other changing quarters acceptable, however dark or gloomy or deteriorating they may be.

The runner who hasn't gone through a survival program that has taught him to do without toilets and showers is in big trouble. Even where there are showers, runners who view hot showers as a must soon learn that they have to finish in the top 10. After that, you take a cold shower or none at all.

For toilets, I have had to search out a friendly gas station owner, or failing that, to do the best I can. Even where accommodations are adequate, local ground rules can sometimes make things difficult. At one race in Central Park, for instance, the crowd of more than 300 runners was allotted three rolls of toilet paper. "People come in and steal it," our friendly park department man kept explaining. It took a near-rebellion to change his mind.

So for most races and many practice runs, my car is still my dressing room. Everything connected with my running is somewhere in that car. It may take a half-hour to find it under all the accumulated shoes and socks and old sweat shirt, but I know it's there.

The one drawback is that this collection has a smell as distinctive in its own way as any created by Chanel. This may be the reason this long distance runner not only runs alone but also rides alone.

O f all the body functions, passing urine is the greatest waste of time. It delays, obstructs and hinders, and does so at the most inopportune times. A bowel movement can be satisfying, especially when you get along in life. An elderly lady who was temporarily residing in a nursing home confirmed this. "All they talk about here," she told me, "is their grandchildren and their last bowel movement."

Emptying the bladder, however, is rarely the topic of conversation, except perhaps as a complaint. It is a nuisance, an interruption of purposeful activity. Children understand this and put it off to the very last second. For this reason, herding younger members of the family into the bathroom before long

car rides is standard practice. For remarkably similar reasons, this sudden irresistible urge also occurs with age. The "weak kidneys" of my childhood have returned. My visit to the toilet before the ride to my grandfather's has now become the visit to the toilet before the ride to my grandchildren's.

Being a competitive runner has undoubtedly worsened my problem. Urine flow can vary from a trickle to a torrent. Its formation involves the most intricate physiology in the body. It is one of the most skillful things the body does, and to any but the closest observers is the most unpredictable. As a runner, I add to these exquisitely programmed variations in kidney function a diminished nervous control of the bladder due to pre-race excitement.

When this happens—when grandpa the runner has the same childlike intensity, the same inner agitation, the same absorption in his play that his grandchildren have—he is bound to have similar problems with his bladder. He is getting into trouble not because he is growing older but because he is getting younger.

Pit-stops for urination, especially if you are a runner on the way to a race, involve higher mathematics. For one thing, the first call of the bladder occurs at about six ounces and usually can be ignored. The last call comes at approximately 12 ounces and says, "Stop, wherever you are!" Normally, the kidneys form about two ounces an hour, but a quart of fluid taken over a short period of time will pass through the kidneys in an hour. So a runner trying to hydrate his body before driving to a race may find it impossible to make it all the way there without relieving himself.

But knowing this is not the solution. I insist on having my coffee before I leave, and will not give up the cola I sip on the turnpike—despite knowing that the caffeine in the coffee and cola is a diuretic that hastens urine production. I am unable to face life, much less a race, without my coffee and cola.

Eventually, there is no ignoring this biological process, and I make a stop. It is made after much the same procrastination and with much the same reluctance that one brings a car into a gas station when the gauge gets closer and closer to "E." Emptying bladders and filling gas tanks are the most useless of my daily actions. I put them off until absolutely necessary.

My relief, however, is only temporary. The kidneys go on producing urine at a marvelous rate so that a half-hour later I am again possessed with this urgency to void. Only now I am on an open meadow, standing with a hundred or more runners. The only cover within miles is a waist-high trash basket.

But when you've gotta go, you've gotta go. I make myself as inconspicuous as possible and nonchalantly go ahead. When taunted I simply answer, "Wait until you're my age."

I refuse to be embarrassed. I learned that early in the distance running game. Years ago, when the Boston marathon was more of a private club than a national event, I was kept with the 200 or so other entrants in a snow-fence stockade on the Hopkinton Commons for about 15 minutes before the race. Hundreds of townspeople and friends surrounded the enclosure, watching us warm up. When my desire to urinate became uncontrollable, I finally asked a veteran how to handle the problem.

He pointed to a runner, calmly urinating in full view of the spectators. "That's a Yale professor over there," he said. "If he can do it, we all can."

It is axiomatic that a runner should compete on an empty stomach. It is equally true that he should go to the line with an empty colon. Yet the athlete gets plenty of advice on his pre-event meal and little or none on his pre-event bowel movement. He is told what and when to eat to ensure an empty stomach, but not told what and when to eat to ensure an empty colon.

Just why a full stomach and a full colon interfere with performance is not well understood. Certainly there are few things more psychologically distressing than running while feeling bloated and distended. But there seem to be definite physiological disturbances as well.

Fortunately the runner has two allies that help his pre-race catharsis: (1) apprehension, and (2) the gastro-colic reflex. The effect of apprehension and anxiety on the gut has been well documented. Such reports go back to the biblical account of the Assyrians' charge and its effects on the gastrointestinal tracts of the Israelites. The classic work, however, is Dr. Walter Alvarez's *Nervousness, Indigestion and Pain,* a fascinating collection of case histories where fear and anxiety and embarrasment and other emotions caused incapacitating abdominal disorders, including diarrhea and distention.

The runner, therefore, should have no difficulty evacuating his colon. The mere anticipation of the race is ordinarily enough to cause a bowel movement. The long lines at the toilet facilities at most marathons attest to this fact.

Where this is not sufficient, the runner should take steps to manipulate the gastro-colic reflex and set it into action. This is a reflex whereby a propulsive movement of the colon is triggered by stimulation of the stomach. One of the best methods of doing this is the morning cup of coffee. Obviously, the coffee does not traverse the 30 feet or so of intestines and cause the bowel movement. It just sends the message. In fact, almost all foods introduced into the stomach will set the colon into motion.

Unfortunately, some foods not only set up this reflex, they cause cramps and diarrhea. It comes down, therefore, to trial and error. And the runner is bound to have a few catastrophies before he establishes a predictable routine. At one point, I thought I had arrived at the perfect pre-race schedule for me: a quart of orange juice and a quart of skimmed milk.

Fortified with this, I ran a good marathon. So I took the same feeding before a nine-mile cross-country race a few weeks later. I had a satisfactory movement before the race started and was two miles into the woods when I developed an uncontrollable diarrhea. I finally had to stop and let my pants down and perch on a rock while the rest of the field streamed past.

I am still working on my problem. I expect little help from physicians. They know little about diet. While I wait I am sticking to my regular day-to-day diet, and depending on my natural cowardice and a cup of coffee to do the rest.

I can put up with Madison Avenue using athletes to promote beer and cigarettes and even men's perfume, but when I see athletes in commercials for anti-perspirants and deodorants, I rise in protest.

It just makes no sense. The athlete wants or needs no anti-perspirant, no deodorant. He is a hitting, throwing, running, jumping advertisement for sweat. Good honest sweat. The kind of sweat that made America and now has virtually disappeared from the country. The kind of sweat that went down the drain with the advent of an affluent technology and the rise of the service industries. The kind of sweat that was eliminated when our occupations turned from action to conversation. The kind of sweat that makes distance runners and middle linebackers and catchers and heavyweight boxers. The kind of sweat that comes from those three million eccrine glands in order to dissipate heat when a person goes into prolonged purposeful action.

For this kind of sweat, you need no deodorant. Honest sweat has no odor. The sweat that comes with effort and exertion, from running hills and bases and slants off-tackle is a dilute salt solution of mint purity. It has a salty, not unpleasant taste and in fact its chemical composition has been duplicated in a drink now being used extensively by marathon runners. There is, therefore, no reason to worry about honest sweat covering your body or saturating your clothes. A daily change of clothes and that old-time favorite, the Saturday night bath, should be all anyone needs.

I have found this to be true for myself. Almost every day in the early afternoon, I change from my street clothes into my running gear and put in a sweaty hour on the roads. At the end of the run I towel off, put my clothes on and go back to work. No shower. Showers are time-consuming and can lead to a chill and all the complications thereof. Showers are also unnecessary if they are used simply to rinse a dilute odorless salt solution off your body.

So what is this billion-dollar deodorant industry up to? Who is their constituency? Who needs these double-strength anti-perspirant deodorants the hucksters are peddling? The answer is simple: the guy watching the commercial, the guy with a top-heavy mortgage, rebellious kids, irritable boss and depressed wife, the guy with nervous sweat.

Nervous sweat comes from the apocrine glands which are relatively few in number and are situated in certain hair-bearing areas like the armpit. These glands go into action at the instant of any emotional distress. They can be triggered by any crisis, be it at home or on the job. Their secretion may bear an odor itself, but in any case provides an excellent culture medium for odor-forming bacteria. The irony of the whole thing is that the apocrine glands are vestigal organs, which means that anatomists don't know why we have them. They have no apparent function in the human, but like the appendix we still have to contend with them.

One way to contend with them is to get rid of the trigger mechanisms of fear and anxiety and guilt and apprehension. And one of the better ways to do this is to work up an honest sweat. The ensuing relaxation and feeling of wholeness, of being in touch with yourself, can bring you safely through confrontations that would ordinarily set the apocrine glands into action. Just when I am about to punch the next person I see right in the nose, I take my daily run and return full of sweetness and light. And this feeling persists at least until it is time to go home and put the clown costume away for another day.

Y ou can't take a shower any time you want. The hot shower is the final act of a ritual, the culmination of a totally exhausting body-mind experience. To take one without the proper preparation is as gross as eating when you're not hungry or drinking when you're not thirsty.

I have some evidence for this wild theory. A *Sports Illustrated* article by the late Yukie Mishima, the Japanese poet and novelist, said the feel of a hot shower after vigorous exercise was one of the elements essential to man's happiness. He summarized it this way:

"Athletics exert man's strength to the utmost. To run and leap, to dart about with sweat pouring from your body, to expend your last ounce of energy and afterward to stand beneath a hot shower—how few things in life can give such enjoyment!"

In most instances, the hot shower puts the seal on a great effort. You have to put pain, agony and exhaustion together to get the great shower. A college football coach once said if there was a heaven on earth it was a locker room after a victory. I'd amend that to a hot shower after agonizing effort.

The hot shower has no more to do with getting clean and odor-free (except maybe symbolically) than the marathon has to do with running an errand. They are both beautiful, purposeless activities which bring man back to his body and are incomplete without each other.

Part II

THE DOCTOR

Seven

Doctors and Health

The annual physical examination has been called a useless annual fiasco. I'll drink some Gatorade to that. You can no more give people health than you can give them wisdom. Society can and must guarantee access to educational opportunity and health services, but learning and health are personal responsibilities.

The main problem with these exams is that the doctor is most concerned with disease. He gives a patient "a clean bill," meaning that all tests are normal. He ignores the fact that the patient is actually physically unfit and even a potential candidate for serious disease.

All American males, for instance, are candidates for heart disease—now generally recognized as the greatest health threat in any industrialized society. And overweight, lack of exercise, high blood pressure, smoking and a high cholesterol increase their chance of having a heart attack by 10 times.

Dr. Donald Cooper, an expert on *Flabiosus Americanus* (the Flabby American), says that no more than 2% of our population gets enough exercise to keep anywhere near physically fit. Which means that 98% of those who wave to me while I'm running on the roads are in trouble and heading for an early old age.

Dr. Tenley Albright, former Olympic gold medalist in women's figure skating and now a Boston surgeon, wrote that sports should teach the medical profession a great deal. Mostly, she said, it should make the physicians realize that normal is not just average. True normal is really the equivalent of a well-trained, physically fit athlete—the obvious example of the human body at its maximum efficiency.

The annual physical, then, should look for fitness rather than disease.

A iling athletes are, other than their present complaint, apparently in fine physical shape compared to the run-of-the-mill spectator. Further, they have unrivaled motivation to get well.

With all this going for them, athletes should be a prime example of our medical establishment's ability to decrease disability and restore health. Unfortunately, they are a prime example of the medical establishment's failure to accomplish either purpose. The prolonged ailments of our top athletes, their recurrent injuries and their slow response to treatment, are all too common feature stories on the sports pages. Forced retirements of star athletes are so numerous, few seem to quit for any other reason.

If athletes were given less care and more thought, the doctors might come up with some original ideas on why illness persists, why injury doesn't clear up. If more non-physicians—podiatrists and physiotherapists, for instance—could be induced to lend their ideas and talents, we might see a completely new approach to sports medicine. And if the athlete had to wait longer for surgery, he might have time to recover from his ailments.

What I'm saying is that medicine, and particularly sports medicine, cannot be let to drift along with the traditional deference we give to the physician and his supposed infallibility. In medicine, this takes the form that physicians alone possess the truth. The profession that learned from a soldier how to treat gout, from a sailor how to keep off scurvy, from a milkmaid how to prevent smallpox and from a Jesuit how to treat malaria now requires that you have an M.D. behind your name before it will listen to you.

But then we are all part of this credential society. We honor the man with titles. We yield at every turn to the expert. We make the degrees behind a man's name determine his credibility. We allow each nation, each discipline, each specialty to set up its idea of Absolute Truth.

Take, for example, our reaction to acupuncture. Physicians schooled in their own dogma reacted with disbelief. Acupuncture violated the doctrines of neuroanatomy, and therefore was impossible, heretical and a delusion.

The fact of the matter is that acupuncture works. Why it works we don't know, any more than we know why a lot of things work. But it works and that should make physicians just that much more receptive to ideas that originate outside of the lecture halls of the medical school.

The fact that acupuncture works, however, is of little importance, even though the public now looks on it as a new panacea. It is simply one more method of relieving pain, one more heroic diversion from the task at hand—which is finding those rules of health which will prevent disease in the athlete.

We now know that the tremendous stresses of training and competition cause injury and disease, but only in the susceptible athlete. That susceptibility, either in (a) structure, as in inherently weak feet, or (b) function, as with weak hamstring or abdominal muscles, must be diagnosed if we are to progress beyond the patchwork, shore-up, make-do medicine that is being practiced today.

To do this, we need doctors willing to think and patients willing to work. Health, like excellence in any form, comes from the individual's own efforts. The doctor who doctors best is a thoughtful spectator to this process.

Sooner or later, it's bound to happen. The general manager of a faltering ball club will call a press conference and the reporters will flock in to hear the field manager get the axe. The high hopes of spring training have collapsed, dashed on the grim realities of July and August. The team has never reached its potential.

But then the general manager starts talking, and a guy in the back of the room asks his neighbor, "Did I hear right? They're firing the doctor?"

He will have heard right. On that fateful day, both club-owners and fans will have reached the conclusion that a losing season may not be entirely the fault of the manager. He may instead be hampered by a roster shot through with injured and unavailable athletes.

The doctor responsible for fielding 25 healthy men every day is the one who has blown his assignment, and he must pay the price. Injuries, which we now see as a most vital consideration in the team's success or failure, are the responsibility of the team doctors. And from the stats I see in the sports news, they are doing a poor job. There is hardly a team that hasn't been minus a key man most of the season, and many have had whole platoons out of action at one time.

Injuries are still being treated with pills and shots and other labor-saving devices. These items have very little to do with returning a player to fighting shape. A pulled muscle is a weak muscle (or else it wouldn't have pulled) and should be strengthened, not cuddled and massaged and heated to jelly.

What we need now are men specializing in the restoration of human beings to optimum muscular function. In medical parlance, this is called rehabilitation, and the doctors who do it are called "physiatrists." Unfortunately for athletes, physiatrists are as rare as .400 hitters. And to make matters worse, few are interested in athletics.

That attitude could easily be changed. Treating athletes is one of the most satisfactory things a doctor can do. They will persist in any treatment no matter how painful or difficult, and in the end the doctor has the satisfaction of seeing a human being performing at the top of his physical powers.

Too much is being done now for the relief of pain. Pain is something a doctor should welcome. It tells him that somehow the whole experiment has gone wrong. Elimination of pain by pills and shots and heat treatments diverts the physician from the task at hand, which is to return to the starting point and begin again at the beginning.

When they finally fire a doctor, we may get the beginning sports medicine needs.

The athlete who consults a physician often wonders what goes on in medical school. He begins to question the priority of disease and disaster, the emphasis on crisis and catastrophe. His own problems of health and preventive medicine, of maximum performance and day-to-day living, seemed to have been ignored.

Physicians who handle emergencies with eclat, who dive fearlessly into abdomens for bleeding aneurysms, who think nothing of managing cardiac arrest and heart failure, who miraculously reassemble accident victims, are helpless when confronted by an ailing athlete. They are even less able to counsel the athlete and his never-ending questions about health.

Health is what makes the athlete medicine's most difficult patient. It is as simple and as complicated as that. Health, said Chesterton, is the mystical and mysterious balance of all things by which we stand up straight and endure. Athletes want that mystical balance by which they can do all things. They want that mysterious harmony of body and spirit which they have come to know as fitness. And because no one man can give them that, because no one man can specialize in health, which is to specialize in the universe, the athletes overwhelm any physician who presumes to treat them.

The athlete needs a medical team to treat him. A team composed not only of physicians but also of professionals from all the health science fields. The physician educated in isolation from these colleagues is usually unaware of the contributions these people can make, and is unwilling to give them authority and autonomy in caring for patients. The physician still sees himself as a member of an elite group in which some members are more elite than others.

A recent poll taken by Professor Stephen Shortell of the University of Chicago makes this perfectly clear. Physicians asked to rate the status and prestige of 41 professional categories in the medical health field ranked no other professional group above any of the medical specialties. They gave first place to the

thoracic surgeons and listed 22 more varieties of doctors before coming to dentists. The physicians seemed particularly ignorant of the importance of podiatrists (40th), who were placed below nurse's aides, or osteopaths (37th), who were given a niche just above practical nurses.

The result is, as the British therapist James Cyriax points out, "Huge numbers of relievable disorders in otehwise healthy people are not relieved, not because nothing can be done but there is no one to apply knowledge already there for the asking."

Who is there, then, who will save us, the athletes and potential athletes? Who is there to bring these specialists up and down the Shortell list together in one complete team dedicated to the nation's health?

I nominate the family practitioner. He is the one man who could orchestrate the whole of patient care, the one man who is close to patients and colleagues, the one man who could come to know the contributions of the other medical health care professionals. He is one generalist among all the specialists.

The physicians place the family practitioner 22nd, at the dividing line between their medical establishment and the professions they consider subordinate to them. I see this primary-care physician as the one man who can unite the medical profession and the others in the health sciences. He alone can go anywhere on this 41-category scale to get help. Freed from the ego problems of the experts whose reputations depend on success, he can advise and counsel and let others take on the onus of the specialist's infallibility.

A thletes have already done a thorough job of raising the consciousness of physicians interested in sports. They have, among other contributions: (a) established a new normal for man; (b) changed our concept of aging; (c) confirmed the idea of the totality of man, and (d) shifted the emphasis from disease to health.

Before we discovered that athletes were attaining maximum metabolic, muscular and cardiopulmonary steady states, we were using "average" individuals as normals. We were, in effect, using life's spectators instead of life's competitors, and were coming up with overweight, out-of-breath subjects testing well below their potential. This can clearly be shown by comparing these pseudo-normals to the athletes in their age group. Their test results are frequently as much as 50% below the athletes' performance.

One effect of this poor performance is to consider early aging as a natural process. Athletes are beginning to make physicians take a new look at this judgment. "The average man," reports Dr. John Naughton after analyzing peak oxygen intakes of 213 men from the ages of 20-55, "becomes physiologically old early in life, which may explain how many succumb to disease of chronic deterioration at an early age." What we now call aging is actually disease.

The athlete has also proven that this exercise and dieting and the resultant fitness has an effect on all our processes—mental and psychological as well as physical. He is making philosophers re-think the body-mind problems which have been with us since the 17th century when Descartes divorced the soul from the body.

This total effect of physical fitness—the new body image, the new self-respect, the new confidence—led Dr. Roger Bannister to describe it as "a state of mental and physical harmony which enables someone to carry on his occupation to the best of his ability and with great happiness."

What Bannister is describing is a state of health that can be quantified by tests of physical fitness, by tests of muscular endurance and strength and speed and percent body fat. But it is also a quality, a method of living. To tell a healthy person not to abuse his body is as unnecessary as telling a saint not to steal. Health is really a form of behavior, a trait like honesty and a way of pursuing one's goals in life.

"Health," says Dr. Bob Hoke, a specialist in occupational medicine, "is a living response to one's total environment."

Health, then, is not merely the absence of disease just as sanctity is not merely the absence of sin. Health is man adapting, man striving, man living the present and thrusting himself into the future. Sport allows us to see purely this living to the utmost, or at least the attempt to do so.

"If there is one statement true of every living person," writes William Schultz, the author of *Joy*, "it must be this: he hasn't achieved his full potential."

The athletes whose efforts have taken him beyond our pedestrian ideas of normal and average and aging and disease sees this quite clearly. Unimpeded by the mediocrity of our vision, he moves toward a horizon where men will make the most of themselves and their world.

Eight

Medicine and Sports

What nature really abhors is complexity. She strives for simplicity, and runs the universe on principles and laws that can be reduced to a few short equations. The universe is, therefore, a seamless whole which we educated specialists have cut up into innumerable unintelligible pieces. And the more we focus down on particulars, the more we concentrate on facts, the more we narrow our line of sight, the less we understand how it all works.

Take the simple process of running. When I began running, I was an educated specialist who concentrated on one area of the human body. I was an expert who relied on other experts for advice.

I soon needed it. Although my ancestors could run forever, my limits were quickly reached. Serious running led swiftly to a series of foot, leg, knee and low-back injuries which threatened to end my new-found happiness on the roads.

I went dutifully to my specialist friends and found to my surprise that they were of little help. They were preoccupied with giving relief to my aching foot, my swollen knee and my throbbing sciatic nerve. They treated the effect, not the cause. And when I resumed running, back came my misery and pain. Clearly, I needed someone more sophisticated, some super-specialist. I had not gone high enough on the specialist ladder to find the wise man to help me.

I soon discovered there was no such wise man. I needed what Bucky Fuller calls a comprehensivist, someone who, childlike, still sees the world as something to be understood, who sees the world as reacting to a few basic laws and principles and who knows that everything that needs to be known is inside of us ready to be drawn out.

When you think this way, you know that running is as natural as breathing. If, therefore, running is routinely accompanied by injury, there must be some deviation from the natural state. The barefoot child, the barefoot native, has no foot or leg trouble. The foot used constantly on dirt or grass or sand transmits only pleasant messages to the tendons and muscles and bones and joints up above. There is no such state as overuse.

It is only when we wear shoes and run on hard flat surfaces that the foot begins to disintegrate.

Almost equally unnatural is the specialization in the one repetitive action of distance running. The native and the child engage in all activities with their legs. They run backwards and sideways, and jump and leap about. In this way, all the muscles are exercised and kept in natural balance. With me, it was quite different. The strong muscles on the back of my legs and back got stronger and shorter as the front muscles and the abdominal muscles got weaker and weaker.

Now I know my body and what is happening to it. I exercise my muscles. I have duplicated that absent dirt and sand in modeling inserts for my shoes. And the shoes I wear have a shank and sole that counteracts some of the attrition of the hard flat surface.

But most of all, I listen to my body and try to unlearn being an educated specialist. It's a lifetime work, this becoming a simple and seamless whole.

If you have heart disease, should you take it easy? Not on your life, according to Dr. Terence Kavanaugh, the director of a cardiac rehabilitation unit in Toronto. In 1973, Kavanaugh had eight of his exercising post-coronary patients increase their running to an average of 50 miles a week and then took them to the Boston marathon. Everyone finished except Kavanaugh.

The Toronto cardiologist is a prime example of a new trend in medicine—prescribing sports instead of drugs. Where once heart disease would disqualify a person from athletics, now more and more physicians see it as a compelling reason to participate. Where once the examining doctor looked for heart disease and high blood pressure and diabetes and asthma and the like to exclude people from sports, the same physician is now urging these same patients to play.

It makes good sense. Illness or not, the individual must try to maximize himself. He must seek his optimum function, physically, psychologically and spiritually. In so doing, he becomes more and more the person he is. This natural health of mind and body comes from inside, not outside, and to attain it the patient needs advice, not medicine. The best advice is very simple: "Be an athlete!"

There was a time when our existence depended on being an athlete. Simple day-to-day living called on all of man's adaptive functions, required no less than physical excellence.

For the great majority of us, that state no longer exists. Today's rigors are entirely different. Exposure in this environment is exposure to tensions and aggravation, to anxiety and guilt and anger and boredom. It is exposure to sugar and salt and alcohol and cigarettes. It is exposure to superficial goals and unrewarding achievements. It is exposure to what is destructive and not purifying. It is exposure to things to which there is no adaptation.

Today's diseases are the interaction of a susceptible individual with that destructive environment. The athlete, on the other hand, returns to the original struggle for life. He returns to a discipline which protects him from affluence and its effects, to competition which is free from guilt and self-destruction, to physical excellence which restores his self-image and corrects his life-style.

The presence of illness or disease only accentuates the need for these activities. If disease is, in part, due to the environment, we must act against that environment. And the first act is action. The less the body does, the less it can do. The muscles set into motion all the adaptive mechanisms of the heart, the respiratory system, the liver, the kidneys, the pancreas, the sweat glands, the endocrine glands and the nervous system.

This also sets in motion emotional and psychological and spiritual events which are less easily charted but equally important. As we return to fitness, to a state where we are bone and muscle and no more, we also remove the psychological and spiritual fat which had contributed to our bloated lives and our bloated self-image.

When the patient becomes an athlete, he accepts the discipline that sport imposes. What he eats, how much he sleeps, are seen as adding to or detracting from his full capability. He also recognizes that however handicapped he is, his limits are much, much higher than he suspected.

"Do your best" applies to diabetics as well as All-Americans. "Become the person you are" is directed to asthmatics as well as world record holders. "Fulfill your design" is meant for heart patients as well as Olympians.

There were always people around complaining about progress, wishing they were back in the good old days—people who think splitting the atom was a tragic mistake, regard the moon shots as a waste of time, and wish the Boston marathon would reduce its field to a few top athletes.

My view is just the opposite. Today, or perhaps tomorrow, is the good old days. Atomic physics has turned scientists into theologians. The Apollo program has turned engineers into ecologists. And the Boston marathon has turned ordinary men into athletes.

The astronauts are obvious examples of the human body at maximum efficiency. They have a live-in physician, in command of some impressive and sophisticated hardware that measures all their functions that are vital, and some that aren't. NASA has discovered that its most delicate instruments are its own astronauts.

The astronauts' physical aim is survival. The marathoner is seeking excellence. Making the 234,000 miles from Cape

Kennedy to the Plains of Descartes and back requires the best medical science can offer. But the 26.22 miles of a marathon are no less demanding, and there are lessons to be learned there that can be taught nowhere else.

Few observers, however, are impressed by the marathon as a research laboratory. In place of the electronic marvels of aerospace medicine and its corps of white-coated professional personnel, the runner is met by a casual volunteer physician who gives him a 10-second interview with a stethoscope applied to his chest.

All the runner gets from this agent of Mission Control is, "Good luck. Next." No one wires him to prevent catastrophe. No one monitors his pounding heart. No one observes his brain waves or sends instructions about his next meal. He is alone in space without instruments, knowing nothing about disastrous changes in his salt and water supplies, unaware of impending circulatory collapse, ignorant of alarming elevations of his lactic acid.

But, instruments or not, the long distance runner is learning. He is learning, for instance, that running these great distances is not simply a matter of talent and training. The race is not always, or even frequently, to the swift. Disaster awaits those who think all it takes to run a marathon is a slow heart, lean body, strong legs—and lots of free time.

With primitive tools and methods, distance runners are learning to avoid things that stand in the way of excellence, and to pick up the things which promote it.

The distance runner knows now that one thing he needs is good feet, and in the absence of that the proper shoes. He knows his training must start months ahead—everyone knows that—but also that too much training is worse than not enough. He is finding, too, what heat can do to him and how to neutralize its effect.

This and more the marathoner has learned: the value of a three-day sugar and starch binge just prior to a race; the danger of a fast start, and the feeling that something very special is happening inside of him.

Most significantly, he's learning that these things happen in predictable patterns. They've always happened that way, but it has only been recently that he has seen what these patterns are. Now, he's in a position to control the odds—to make running more a science and less a gamble.

The runner in search of excellence has discovered what Einstein did—that "God doesn't play dice with the world."

The most important medical book of this century was not about disease. It was an account of research into the function of the emotions written by Walter B. Cannon in 1915 and called *Bodily Changes in Pain, Hunger, Fear and Rage.*

The book was based on Cannon's thesis: "The bodily changes that accompany great excitement are directed toward efficiency in physical struggle." An individual can tap enormous reserves when the emotions (Cannon called them "energizing mechanisms") are called into action.

Now we need an addition to Cannon's work, another medical classic that is not about disease but about the development of human potential in much more logical and systematic ways. It could be called, *Bodily Changes with Exertion, Environment, Diet and Constitution.* And it should be based on the theory that there are unexplored ways for each one of us to be stronger and faster and more durable.

As with any exploration of man's world, be it physical or intellectual, psychological or spiritual, this hunt is not without danger. Cannon's work uncovered the adverse as well as the beneficial effects of emotions. He showed that feelings, when misdirected, are the cause of psychosomatic disease. So too the athlete pushed beyond his capabilities will develop the illnesses of "overuse"—what we could call "the diseases of excellence." These diseases of today's athletes will be the diseases of tomorrow's common man, when increasing leisure will open up humanity's possibilities—which is why sports medicine is the medicine of the future.

As of now sports medicine (and indeed all of medicine) resembles nothing more than a giant spy network in which no one has the master plan. Everyone is working out his little coded message in complete isolation, with no idea of what others are contributing to the solution. The result is a system going nowhere. And even where there is movement, it is in the wrong direction. Sports medicine remains a source of frustration to both physician and patient. No Walter Cannon has come along with his vision of the big picture, with his ability to gather diverse facts from many fields and put them together.

Despite this we are making progress. The world's records of 20 years ago are the high school records today. The human body is not only the greatest marvel in the world, it is getting more marvelous as standards of living improve.

But marvel or not, there are limits. We will continue to push them back, but they cannot be ignored. They must be treated with respect. The man trying to become a whole man must be aware that he has hidden weaknesses and susceptibilities. "There is a crack in everything God made," wrote Emerson. And it will reveal itself under stress.

This may sound pretentious to anyone who simply wants a doctor to take care of his tennis elbow or heel spur or aching knee. But no elbow or heel or knee is an island. Everything is connected to everything else, and is related to the total person.

The athlete with these problems has been described as a person who tries to get the most out of his genetic endowment through training in his environment. These training methods are based on Selye's General Adaptation Syndrome, the application of increasing loads with appropriate rest intervals.

These programs are, in effect, gross testing of every system in the body. They stretch the athlete physically, psychologically and spiritually. Each athlete, therefore, is an experiment-of-one who needs an individualized schedule which includes sleep, diet and practice sessions. Otherwise, he will get his badge of honor, a disease of excellence.

Unfortunately, given the present state of the art, he is likely to get the disease before he arrives at the excellence.

Would you believe there are people in America in trouble from trying too hard? This information, however implausible, happens to be true. And not a mere handful of dedicated nuts. All over the country, runners, tennis players, football and baseball players, golfers and athletes of all description—pro, amateur, weekend and what have you—are consulting their physicians because of symptoms due to trying too hard.

The first wave of these patients caught the medical profession by surprise. Doctors are accustomed to seeing man's attempt to maximize himself—but only for ill. They are adjusted to a fat, indolent clientele.

This gloomy group, however, has become interspersed with an odd bunch who come to the office because of foot, leg, arm and other pains due to excessive activity. "It all began," the patient will say, "after I started running 100 miles a week." Or, "I'd been averaging three hours of tennis a day without trouble when I changed my racket." Or, "I wonder if 36 holes three times a week is too much."

Medics trained to disease rather than overuse confront these self-maximizers in disbelief, and are unable to give any advice except to cease and desist from such foolishness. This is a unsatisfactory prescription for any athlete, but especially disappointing to one passionate enough to devote the amount of time necessary to develop this type of ailment.

That amount of time has been estimated to be five times what athletes put into training prior to World War II. Distance runners, because of the success of the revolutionary ideas of Arthur Lydiard, are running up to 20 miles a day—a distance during which each foot strikes the ground 17,000 times. No wonder any number of "overuse syndromes" occur in this category of athletics. No surprise, therefore, that we have to deal with stress fractures, shin splints, fallen arches, achilles tendinitis. If even a microscopic difficulty is repeated 17,000 times, something has to give.

Nine

Stress and Rest

In the winter of 1940, when I was a senior at Manhattan College, I won both the mile and half-mile races in one of those numerous armory meets held during the New York indoor season. My times were the best I had ever run, and the entire performance drew a mention from Jesse Abramson in the *Herald-Tribune* the next day. The following week, I felt tired. I never ran another good race while I was in college.

Three decades later, I set a US mark for my age in the two-mile and came back to win the mile an hour or so later. The next day, I won a 50-and-over five-mile race. I felt tired for months after that.

The story is a familiar one whenever coaches and runners talk about the mysteries of running. A personal best performance, another push to the limits and then disaster. Being at absolute peak is just one step away from losing it all, and usually it is the old sin of pride, that extra race, which triggers the destruct button.

The urge toward excellence can breed arrogance—a feeling that you are superior to the laws of nature. The athlete's sin is no minor one like lust or envy or greed. The apple of being all you can be, and being it *now*, is almost impossible to resist.

For some, recovery follows in a week or two of inactivity. For others, months go by before they are able to run with competence and zest. This is bad enough, certainly, but how many runners are lost to the sport forever? How many athletes, not knowing what is going on, push themselves harder and harder as their running deteriorates, and finally give up on the sport for which they were most fitted?

My guess is that the number is enormous. This staleness and poorly treated musculo-skeletal problems are the major causes of quitting running. The question, therefore, is can we anticipate these breakdowns and somehow forestall them and the subsequent defections? Is there a way to prevent these depressing and incapacitating events?

Yes, one way is to understand and work with GAS. The General Adaptation Syndrome is a three-phase formula of stress and its effects first outlined by Canadian physiologist Hans Selye. It is based on the common and easily observable fact that man exposed to an unaccustomed strenuous task goes through three stages: experiences a hardship, then gets used to it, and finally can't stand it any longer—or as Selye terms the sequence, (1) alarm, (2) resistance, (3) exhaustion.

Translated into training, this means applying increasing amounts of work (Stage 1) with a resultant improvement in performance (Stage 2) but stopping before exhaustion (Stage 3). The coach and his athletes must know that peak ability means exhaustion and staleness are close at hand.

The moral is simple: The next time you run out of GAS, fill up your tank with rest.

The main worry of the competitive runner is not injury but overtraining. The runner knows the race is as easily lost by training too much as by doing too little, by trying too hard rather than not enough, and by going too far with the Nietzschean wager, "What doesn't destroy me makes me strong."

The Italians, who have made a science of observing this destructive phenomenon in their beloved bicyclists, call it *sur-manage*. We call it staleness or overtraining or peaking too soon. The causes are many and vary for each athlete, but Nietzche's dictum still holds. A stress is applied and the body reacts. If it adapts, the body is stronger. If it fails to adapt, it is destroyed. To prevent such catastrophes, the process must be caught in the early stages, at which time a cure is still possible.

Unfortunately, the early symptoms are quite vague: lack of enthusiasm, decrease in interest, tiredness and irritability are complaints all too common for most of us from time to time. The runner may also notice a shortened attention span, difficulty in studying, trouble with staying asleep at night, a drop in grades. And during this time, he becomes more liable to develop allergies as well as colds and strep throats and mononucleosis. There is an increased susceptibility to inflammation and infection.

All this may alert the runner that something is amiss. But the first definite sign of staleness he may recognize is a poor performance. If so, it is already too late to do much. The runner will now have to spend weeks and even months getting back to the peak he has just passed.

The best treatment, therefore, is prevention, and the absolute essential for prevention is what horse trainers call (1) "bottom," 8-10 weeks of endurance work. And along with that the runner needs adequate rest. This means (2) eight hours' sleep in early training and nine when the training gets tough. It also means (3) a nap before the afternoon workout.

Next, the runner enters the dangerous six-week period of high intensity interval training that will bring him to his maximum capabilities. These sessions increase his body's ability to use high-energy phosphates and handle lactic acid. They build up his anaerobic capacity which so often is the decisive factor in dividing winners from losers.

He must, however, keep this work within his personal limits. And no coach can tell the runner his appropriate pace as precisely as his own body can. (4) Speed workouts therefore must be individualized.

But even an experienced runner finds listening to his body can be deceptive, he needs (5) more scientific ways of monitoring his progress toward this treacherous zenith on his performance charts. And our Italian friends have provided one.

When you first awaken in the morning, lie quietly in bed for five minutes, then take your pulse. Rise, go to the bathroom, and then weigh yourself. Record both pulse and weight. Following training, shower, weigh and then lie down for 15 minutes (do not sleep), then check pulse. Again, record both pulse and weight. These figures will show if you are training too little, too much or just enough. If your morning pulse is higher than the previous morning, you are not completely rested and should either not train or train lightly. If your weight is also falling, you are overtraining. Your afternoon pulse and weight should get closer and closer to the morning figures as you get nearer and nearer to your peak.

Now the runner is finally ready for (6) his tapering period, 7-10 days of decreasing work to husband his strength, both physical and psychological, for the final assault.

It all sounds so easy. But what about the cross-country runner faced with three three-mile races a week almost as soon as he gets his uniform. Instead of a diet of pure endurance runs, he has these tri-weekly high intensity equivalents of six interval halves at 2:30-2:35 with no rest in between. And if somehow he escapes peaking prematurely under this program (and the interval halves his coach adds on), he is faced with six championship races in a row. *Sur-manage* is the inevitable result.

When Don Schollander was in training for the 1964 Olympics, he was faced with the prospect of three major tests in a row: the national championships at the end of July, the Olympic Trials at the end of August, and six weeks later the Olympics themselves.

"Physically and psychologically," he wrote, "it was impossible to peak for all three." He decided, therefore, to take a chance and ease off in the Trials where he took two second places to qualify for the team.

Few spectators realize the truth of Schollander's statement. They assume that the athlete comes each week to the competition more or less in the same condition. That condition,

they think, is maintained by training methods which are standard, and result in permanent peak condition and performance. The runner, to them, is the world's equivalent of the "top gun." He must win every time out or they will begin to say, as they did of Schollander, "Is he going downhill? Is he clutching under pressure?"

Unfortunately, runners and coaches, raised on the American tradition of either testing themselves against the top guns or maintaining their own position as top guns, ask themselves the same question. The final result of such constant affronts to man's physical and psychological capabilities is just such a debacle as occurred in the 1972 Olympic Trials in Eugene, Ore.

In the 800-meter trials, the three fastest Americans of the past year—Tom Von Ruden, Juris Luzins, and Mark Winzenried—were eliminated. The trio had held starring roles through the indoor season, traveling from coast to coast and frequently running twice a week. Based on their past records, the race at Eugene seemed to be a mere formality before they picked up their tickets for Munich.

But it was not to be. They failed. They had succumbed to a new and unrecognized menace—overracing. The greatest known danger to runners prior to this has been overtraining. The effects of daily practices of grueling intensity and duration have been fairly well documented. And although coaches continue to tread the line which separates fitness from exhaustion, most are fully aware of the hazards.

Overracing, however, is a less evident threat. Moreover, it is insidious. The race, you see, is the love-making of the runner. This is his peak experience. The clock, that unforgiving minute, is there to be tested and enjoyed. So are the other competitors providing the tempo that makes each race so different from the next, and the crowd whose shouts keep you continually keyed up and reaching for your best effort. It is a package few can resist. Von Ruden, Luzins and Winzenried couldn't.

Von Ruden went stale. Luzins' arch acted up. Winzenried came down with achilles tendinitis. Overracing bore its fruit.

As the week in Eugene went by, American coaches were being taught a lesson one of them already knew. Bill Bowerman, the first coach in this country to recognize the dangers of over-training, was also the first to realize the hazards of overracing. And at the Trials his pupils took five of 12 berths in the four longest runs.

How does Bill Bowerman do it? How come that year after year his Oregon runners are the best in the country and frequently the best in the world? What is the Bowerman secret?

His method is simplicity itself. From the lowest level of ability (he has co-authored a book on jogging), he has advocated the hard day-easy day program—a hard day of work and an easy day to recoup. For some, this might even be two easy days. Running should be fun, he thinks. It should be approached with zest, he believes. Very little is to be gained, he states, by torturing yourself.

So Bowerman avoids the overtraining menace, and he has helped his runners resist the lure of overracing. Oregon runners are only rarely seen during cross-country, which Bowerman views as a season for building up the distance man. Races, he claims, interfere with that progress and—even worse—may tear the runner down.

An Oregon runner in an indoor meet is an even rarer event. Bowerman waits for the outdoor season before he gets his men into high gear, pointing toward the later stages of the season. Then and only then all systems are go.

The basic pattern begins to emerge. Bowerman views track as a lifetime activity (Eugene is the "jogging capital") which can be made enjoyable and rewarding year in and year out. And like all human activities it follows the seasons as we build up gradually to a yearly peak performance. We leave that like a mark on a tree to which we return in a year to see how much taller and stronger we've become.

Are you a "sleep cheat"? Are you gradually adding to a sleep deficit night after night? If so, you are in for serious physical and psychological consequences, warns Dr. Julius Segal of the National Institute of Mental Health. Segal is only one of a number of researchers on sleep who are discovering that sleep is one of the essential needs of man. "We sacrifice it," says Segal, "at considerable peril to our bodies and minds."

This is no news to poets, parents and coaches. The people who are really close to what makes for health and happiness and maximum human performance knew this all along. Those whose knowledge of the human condition came from meditation and love and concern realized this long before the experts on physiology and the biological sciences.

The scientists are, as usual, late arrivals. They are only now finding out what Keats meant when he wrote of "a sleep/Full of sweet dreams, and health and quiet breathing."

There are two types of sleep. The first is called "REM" (rapid eye movement) and consists of relatively short periods in which dreams occur. The second type is the orthodox or non-dreaming sleep. This is called "S" (slow-wave) sleep because of changes in the brain waves detectable on the electroencephalogram.

These two types of sleep apparently have different functions. S-type is necessary for biological health and performance. During this type of sleep, the body pours out growth hormone which in adults has the function of promoting the renewal of our tissues. REM sleep, on the other hand, seems to be mainly concerned with psychological function. Without it, we soon get into serious emotional and intellectual difficulties.

But haven't mothers over the centuries known that? Hasn't every one of us been told by our mother that we must sleep to grow? And hasn't the cranky child always been excused by the explanation that he had not had enough sleep? Science is once again confirming the old wisdom.

Science is also confirming the wisdom of the coach's curfew. When an athlete becomes a "sleep cheat," he is upsetting a very delicate balance between applied stress and the body's recuperative powers. Further, in limiting the hormonal repose he may be limiting his own potential in his sport.

Missing curfew has definite consequences on both types of sleep, but particularly on slow-wave sleep. This is of primary interest to the athlete. S-sleep increases after exercise and no doubt contributes to physical conditioning. With it comes an increase in protein synthesis which translates into speed, strength and endurance.

Just what is the optimal sleep length for each individual is unknown. In the early 1500s, Andrew Boode's *Dietary of Health* suggested eight hours in summer and nine hours in winter as the ideal time to sleep. We have not progressed much beyond this suggestion. Surveys suggest that 7½ hours is the average sleep taken by most people.

Most books on health and exercise physiology skirt this problem. They merely suggest "adequate" sleep, as if the individual surely knows his own requirement.

If we could hear what our body is telling us, that might be so. But in a 24-hour society where there is always action somewhere and any number of reasons not to go to bed, our need for sleep goes unnoticed. The call to slumber is ignored. The voice of the body is unheard. Which is why the lack of adequate sleep is a primary problem in the training of athletes.

Nature, you see, makes no allowances for such mistakes. Her penalties for violating the curfew are a lot more substantial than any coach's. And nature's bedchecks occur every night.

My first coach was partial to naps. I took naps to make up for lost sleep, took naps to conquer fatigue and prevent exhaustion, took naps to make me strong and increase endurance. I even took naps to improve my disposition. When things were going wrong and there was any doubt about what to do, I took a nap. And for whatever reason, the nap theory worked. It produced what it promised.

The nap is a biological and psychological and spiritual necessity. It renews and restores and revives. But only in childhood do we accept it. Only in childhood do we use again and again that first 90 minutes of sleep which scientists tell us is the deepest and most refreshing of all.

Yet the nap is the only answer for the overtrained athlete who finds himself more and more fatigued, whose performance is deteriorating, who lacks zest and is losing interest. This athlete is the one who needs more sleep at night, a nap during the day and a halt in his training.

The professional athletes have come to know this. Those athletes who are totally into the use of their bodies, who plan their day around maximum performance, know the importance of rest. I saw in the *New York Times* that basketball player Walt Frazier occasionally sleeps for 18 hours straight when the Knicks are on the road. A survey of touring women tennis pros showed that most of them slept nine or 10 hours a night. I recall also that Tom O'Hara, when he was the leading indoor miler, would sleep for most of the 24 hours preceding a race.

The nap is also the answer to the self-imposed work-play week of the ordinary citizen. Few people are constructed of material strong enough to handle a program which includes a 40-hour work week, commuting, nighttime TV, and a weekend of exhuasting physical and social activities. This life-style leads to what must be the major deficiency disease of our age—a deficiency in rest.

It is the child in me who accepts these demands, who refuses to acknowledge any physical restriction, who pushes on to exhaustion and depression, apathy and despair. But it is also the child in me who knows the answer.

When I become tired and irascible and even more difficult to live with than usual, when there is no zest in running and my races are getting worse and worse, I remember my first coach. And I look around for my baby blanket and a soft spot where I can lie down.

Man's fourth unalienable right is the time-out. This pause, this breather, this break in the action, is what makes life, liberty and the pursuit of happiness possible. Without the time-out, I would not know what life to lead, how to use my liberty or what happiness to pursue. At the moment I forget whence I came, why I am here and where I am going, it is the right to call "Time" that saves me.

I find this truth to be self-evident. I see it every weekend on television. When winning and losing hangs in the balance, when the play gets ragged and the players fatigued, when the game plan has been forgotten and the athletes demoralized, the time-out works wonders. I've seen courage replace fear and purpose take the place of indecision. I've seen teams come back relaxed and composed and confident, all because of the time-out.

And so when I am losing my head and all about me are keeping theirs, when I am filled with the frustrations and anxieties of my daily routine, when I am no longer living my own life but simply reacting to others, I look for a time-out, whether it is 60 minutes or 60 seconds.

That time-out, that hour a day that belongs to me, must remain inviolate. No excuse, no friend, no cause, no duty, can come between me and that hour and whatever I might want to do with it. Mostly I take that hour and run with it, and thereby revive and restore and replenish the man I am.

The 60-second time-outs, on the other hand, cannot be programmed. I take them where I find them. At a stop light, I could fume and sputter about getting there instead of being here. But it is much better to read a book. Or do isometric exercises for my stomach muscles. Or take the opportunity to recharge my senses with colors and odors and sounds, or to see the geometry of the buildings, the pattern of the trees, the movement of the people, or to see familiar objects as if for the first time. And soon my red lights become too short.

Too soon I am being whistled back into the game. Too soon I begin to forget once again I am animal, artist, mystic, clown, that I am really concerned with quite simple things, with things that only come when I finally loose the reins and become calm and relaxed and cease my tense activity, when I stop counting and measuring and comparing and weighing.

Ten

Feet and Legs

I am a cardiologist, but my relationship to sports medicine has been as an athlete rather than a doctor. What I have experienced as a runner—and what judgment I have been able to bring to this experience as a physician—have convinced me that traditional medicine isn't dealing adequately with athlete problems.

In more than 10 years as a distance runner, I have experienced almost every injury of the foot, leg, knee, thigh and back. During that time, the medical profession has only been able to provide me with symptomatic relief. It wasn't until I came under the care of a podiatrist (foot specialist) that I was able to run for prolonged periods and be free of foot, leg and knee difficulties.

Yet the medical profession has been slow in adopting this method of treatment which obviously is effective. The standard treatment of the most common ailment of runners, chondromalacia of the knee (which I call "runner's knee" because the technical term is so clumsy) is a case in point. Runner-patients are still advised to rest, wear casts, try a variety of medications, do quadriceps exercises and, when all else fails, to undergo surgery.

In my first years as medical columnist for *Runner's World,* I made these same suggestions to the victims of runner's knee. There must, you see, be a standard operating procedure—even if it doesn't work.

Meanwhile, I was getting hints that the foot was the cause of it all. A high school runner told me that he had trouble with his knee if he wore a certain pair of shoes. Another runner had pain while using a banked track. I had knee pain and found it was due to the slant of the road. My left knee gave me trouble if I ran with traffic. I cured the pain by running against traffic, and thought no more of it.

No more, that is, until I began a lengthy correspondence with Tom Bache, an ex-Marine and a fine runner in the San Diego area. Tom had suffered from runner's knee for two years when we began to exchange ideas. He had gone through every therapy suggested in the literature (short of surgery), without success. As soon as he got back to running, the pain returned.

I wrote to Tom about the crown-of-the-road idea and about running on the outside of the foot. This helped him until he would forget, get tired or lose form in a race. So his problem continued. Neither Tom nor I thought of the next logical step, foot supports, until his arch started to bother him and he sought help from runner-podiatrist Dr. John Pagliano.

Dr. Pagliano fitted Bache for supports, and *voila!* Tom lost his knee pain and in a matter of weeks was up to marathon training. He ran the best marathon of his career shortly after.

After this experience, I saw the number one man on a local college cross-country team. He had severe symptoms of runner's knee. I looked at his feet, and even to a cardiologist his problems seemed evident. His feet were a disaster area. After podiatric treatment, he returned to running again within a week and was completely asymptomatic.

Soon I was seeing tennis players with the same problem, and hearing about more and more runners who were being helped with drug store supports, and others who had reached to podiatrists for treatment and were back to full-scale running. The treatment was successful not only for knee pain but for the gamut of injuries along the foot-leg chain.

This convinced me that no matter what an athlete's complaint is, we should look first to his feet as the source of the trouble. The foot is an architectural marvel—an engineering masterpiece which has 26 bones, four times as many ligaments, and an intricate network of tendons which act as guy-ropes or slings for the arches. When these components are perfectly balanced, the foot can handle almost any amount of work. However, even a minute deviation from normal can cause adjustments that will eventually produce injury either in the foot, or in its supporting muscles and tendons, or even in the structures above it.

When this happens, we have familiar afflictions such as heel spurs, achilles tendinitis, shin splints, calf pulls, stress fractures and the ubiquitous runner's knee. In sports medicine, these problems are lumped under the category of "overuse syndromes." It was originally felt that excess activity was the sole cause of the trouble, and remedies were directed to relieving discomfort, to allowing a suitable period of rest and then to resuming the training activity.

Unfortunately, the presence of an "X" factor was not suspected and therefore was left uncorrected. Hence, the result of therapy was predictable. The athlete went through a sequence of pain, followed by relief through rest and treatment, and a return of pain when training resumed.

The long-suffering athletes cried, "Why me? Why a good guy like me? Why should I have trouble with my feet (or knees or legs) when my teammates who practice as much as I do have no difficulty?"

The answer is that the ailing athlete has an inherent susceptability to his injury. And this susceptibility, the "X" factor which the medical profession is so slow to recognize, was a structurally weak foot.

When an athlete goes into training, three things can happen to his muscles. Two of them are bad: shortening of the strengthened muscles with loss of flexibility; weakness of the opposing, relatively unused muscles.

"The irony is that the athlete is less fit in regard to flexibility standards than the typical man in the street," writes *Fitness for Living* editor Robert Bahr. "That's because strengthening and endurance exercises act to shorten muscles and reduce flexibility." It is Bahr's belief also that more muscle tears, pulls and and strains occur because of this lack of flexibility.

The best answer to this lack of flexibility is yoga. For one thing, in yoga the stretching is gentle, smooth, non-painful and achieved over a period of time. "Stretching by bobbing or bouncing," writes physiologist Dr. Herbert de Vries, "invokes the stretch reflex which actually opposes the desired stretching."

Yoga or not, the stretching athlete is only halfway home. He has to start strengthening exercises of the weakened antagonist muscles.This will prevent the imbalance in muscle strength that many observers feel is the other major cause of pulls, tears and strains.

"A number of studies have shown," says physiotherapist Joseph Zohar, "That when one muscle group is excessively stronger that the opposing muscle group, the odds of injury in the weaker muscle are greatly increased." The evidence is that an excessively high ratio of strength between the quadriceps (the front thigh muscles) and the hamstrings (the rear thigh muscles) increases the chance of a hamstring pull.

The principle is easy, the application difficult. Each sport strengthens and therefore shortens a different set of muscles. The flexibility problems of a sprinter, for instance, differ from those of the distance runner, as do his muscle imbalances. The distance runner has stronger, shorter hamstrings and therefore tends to pull his weaker quadriceps. The sprinter who uses his quads to explode out of the blocks has weaker hamstrings, and the back of his thigh is where he grabs when he gets that tearing sensation midway in the 100-yard dash.

The main interest of the people in sports medicine is not to predict these events (which some researchers have done by testing athletes) but to prevent them. The biomechanical approach to muscle balance provides just such a program. It is part yoga, part muscle balancing. Zohar calls it preventive conditioning. What it means it that no weakness, no tightness, no muscle imbalance will go uncorrected.

When an athlete trains that way, when he applies engineering and architectural principles to his body, he doesn't have to worry about the two bad things that usually happen. And he may even get some unexpected dividends.

"The balanced conditioning of individual muscle groups," states Zohar, "not only protects the body against injury but also improves its performance to unprecedented levels."

The human body is a marvelous instrument. When in perfect alignment and balance, there is almost no feat of endurance the body cannot handle even on a regular basis. However, structural imbalance of even minor degrees can result in incapacitating injuries and persistent disability. Prevention and treatment of musculoskeletal problems in the athlete, therefore, rests on the establishment of the structural balance and architectural integrity of the body—and its re-establishment should injury occur.

There is very little place in the treatment of these diseases for injections, medications and manipulations. Treatment rests almost completely on the following:

Biomechanical treatment of the foot. This means providing a foot support or orthotic which keeps the foot in proper balance. Ordinarily, this entails the preservation of the neutral position of the foot. What we do is bring the ground up to meet the foot, thus preventing it from flattening or coming over on the inside (pronating).

Flexibility and strengthening of the muscles. Ordinary training involves the continual repitition of one motion and the use of one main axis of muscles. This results in two unwanted effects: (a) shortening and loss of flexibility in the exercised muscle, the prime mover, and (b) weakness in the antagonist which opposes it. Additional exercises are needed to prevent this.

It would be wrong to consider these measures as "either/or". Both are necessary. Biomechanical problems in the foot are accentuated as the muscles tighten and their opposing muscles weaken. Treatment to the muscles, therefore, lessens the required corrections of the feet. Conversely, using orthotics for the shoes can lessen the symptoms due to muscle imbalance in the leg, thigh and back. This is particularly true in instances of the "short-leg syndrome," now thought to be due to muscle spasm and to be helped by both heel lifts and muscle re-education.

Using these general principles, one can move on to a general preventive program. First, the runner must review his feet with three major abnormalities in mind:

Morton's Foot: This is a short first toe with a long second toe. The short first metatarsal tends to pronate the foot and cause failure of the long arch as well. This (and other pronatory influences) can cause such problems as:

1. *Heel spur syndrome.* This is improperly called a heel spur. Actually, it is a fascitis, an inflammation of the plantar fascia which attaches to the heel spur and spreads across the foot like a fan reaching to the toes.

2. *Posterior tibial tendinitis.* This causes pain on the inside of the leg along the shin bone. Sometimes it is mistakenly called shin splints, a term reserved for pain along the front of the leg between the two shin bones.

3. *Chondromalacia or "Runner's Knee."* This causes the pain and occasionally tenderness under the kneecap and sometimes to either side. It results from the foot flattening out and transmitting a torque to the knee, causing the kneecap to ride over on the knob of the thigh bone.

Loss of the long arch. This can cause all of the above.

Unstable heel. This movement can result in achilles tendinitis and "runner's knee."

Prevention for these conditions would include a heel cup, minimal heel lift, a longitudinal arch and a Morton's extension. Judicious use of arch "cookies," heel cups and felt for heel lifts, arch supports and Morton's extensions can be done on a do-it-yourself basis.

Next, the runner should review his muscular status. The

distance runner will shortly find that he has established tightness of the muscles running from his foot to his low back. The achilles will tighten, as will his gastrocnemius, hamstrings and iliopsoas. Meanwhile, his front muscles, the anti-gravity muscles, will become weaker. When this happens, he is in trouble. The difficulties to look for are as follows:

Inflexibility of the achilles. This leads to achilles tendinitis and worsens any biomechanical problem in the foot. It also overbalances the shin muscles and makes them unable to handle stress.

Tightenings of the hamstrings. This contributes to low back and sciatic problems. It also sets the runner up for a quadriceps pull through relative weakness of that group. It contributes to the short leg syndrome.

Shortening of the iliopsoas. This is almost always present in sciatic and low back pain. It also may contribute to the short leg syndrome.

Weakness of any of the opposing muscles, including the anterior chamber muscles (shin splints), quadriceps (quadriceps pull) and stomach muscles (rectus pull), sciatica and low back problems.

Preventive maintenance therefore involves the following: (1) foot care, (2) flexibility exercises, (3) strengthening exercises.

When faced with an injury not due to a collision or a fall, the runner must assume that he is out of structural balance. No medication is going to restore that balance. He must get down to basics, diagnose where he is out of line and correct it. He will get temporary relief with whatever the doctor recommends, i.e., rest, butazolidine, cortisone shots or whatever. But as soon as he resumes running, he will quickly get into trouble again.

With this in mind and remembering what we have said about structural balance, let us consider some of the most frequent running ailments and proposed treatment:

• *Achilles tendinitis:* Cause—short achilles, gastroc, hamstring axis; unstable heel; inverted heel; weak arch; excessive use of toe flexors. Treatment—stretching of achilles; heel lifts, arch supports; anterior crests.

● *Heel spur syndrome:* Cause—no shank in shoes; Morton's foot; weak foot; forefoot varus. Treatment—"doughnut" for heel; full foot orthotic for forefoot problems as well as arch; shoe with good shank (Tiger Corsair, Nike Cortez, Puma 9190, Adidas Country or SL-72).

● *Stress fracture, metatarsal:* Cause—unstable heel; weak arch; other pronatory abnormalities and forefoot problems. Treatment—full foot orthotic with attention to Morton's foot; forefoot varus and unstable heel.

● *Runner's knee:* Cause—pronatory foot influences including the unstable heel, weak foot; forefoot varus and Morton's foot. Treatment—heel stabilizer; arch; possible full foot orthotic.

● *Numbness of the feet* (distance runner's neuropathy): Cause—sciatic nerve pressure. Treatment—stretching of hamstrings and iliopsoas along with abdominal situp (bent leg) and isometric tummy tucking.

● *Other sciatic syndromes,* pain in the thigh and buttock: Cause—tight hamstrings, iliopsoas, weak abdominals. Treatment—use same flexibility and strengthening exercise; use of a Sacrogard belt (usually $6-8 at drugstores).

● *Shin splints:* Cause—weakness of the anterior chamber muscles. Treatment—strengthen muscles by flexing foot with weight over toes; anterior crest to lessen use of flexors stretching for the opposing muscles, the achilles and gastroc and hamstrings.

● *Groin pain:* Cause—unknown but probably a mixture of weakness of the adductor muscles, the short leg syndrome and biomechanical difficulties in the foot. Treatment—advise flexibility exercises along with exercises drawing leg toward the mid-line; attention to any biomechanic problem of the foot, however mild.

We are dealing in problems measured in millimeters. Often the injury is precipitated by wear of the regular training shoe down to a critical point—the heel, for instance, where an eighth of an inch makes the difference. Use of a totally new type of shoe for a major effort will also bring on difficulties, as will change of surfaces and even change of direction when there is a slant in the road.

I cannot emphasize too strongly that this is a structural, almost architectural, problem, not a medical one. You would almost be better off in the hands of an engineer than a doctor when these illnesses strike. At least you would not have your problem complicated by medication which in the long run will do no good. What the runner needs is to be restored to structural balance. Acupuncture, surgery or wonder drug will not do that.

Eleven

Heart and Mind

Is there an athletic heart?

Yes, there is. Athletes have bigger and better hearts than the ordinary person. We have always sensed this. Our heroes have been called mighty-hearted and great-hearted and lion-hearted. The word courage takes its root from the Latin word for heart. Now scientists using echosound to map out the exact dimensions of the heart have been able to prove the athletic heart exists.

How does an athletic heart differ from an average heart?

The studies at the National Heart Institute in Bethesda demonstrated two basic types of athletic hearts: "endurance hearts," found in swimmers and long distance runners, are bigger, "resistance hearts," seen in wrestlers and shot putters, are heavier.

What are the characteristics of the endurance heart?

The emphasis in this heart is on the filling phase or diastole. Endurance training demands a high cardiac output for long periods of time. The heart adapts by increased filling.

In such athletes, the volume at rest may be twice that of the ordinary citizen. Nevertheless, the heart wall does not thicken, but the entire heart grows larger. The largest hearts on x-ray study are those of professional bicyclists, closely followed by marathoners and cross-country skiers.

What are the characteristics of the resistance heart?

Here, it is not the volume of ejection that is important, but the force. Training in these sports is for sudden, severe maximal effort. The time element is relatively brief. As a consequence, the wall thickens while the capacity of the heart changes very little. For this reason, enlargement is not too evident. Hearts of shot putters, gymnasts, weight lifters and normal controls look much the same.

The echo, however, shows the truth of what Harvey wrote in 1628: "The more muscular and powerful the men, the stronger, thicker and denser their hearts." These are hearts that emphasize systole or contraction, while the runner's heart depends on diastole or expansion.

Is the athlete heart normal?

If fitness is normal, the athletic heart is normal. If the ability to work with vigor and pleasure and without undue fatigue is desirable, then the athletic heart is desirable. If we were created to live at the top of our powers, then the athletic heart is necessary for the good life.

Is there any danger with an athletic heart?

The main danger is going to the doctor. Physicians are generally unfamiliar with exercise physiology. They become alarmed at the normal physiological changes that accompany heavy training and peak condition. They are, therefore, likely to give bad advice that could cause an athlete to quit his sport, lose his livelihood and be ineligible for life insurance.

What are these normal "abnormal" findings in a trained athlete?

These occur mostly but not exclusively in endurance hearts: (1) slow pulse—rates can go down as far as 28 beats per minute; (2) irregular pulse—premature beats and heart block; (3) low blood pressure; (4) orthostatic hypotension—the blood pressure goes even lower when the athlete stands up; (5) heart murmurs due to the force and volume of flow; (6) third heart sounds, which under other circumstances suggest a weak heart; (7) abnormal EKGs—the Wilt Chamberlain Syndrome where the heart tracings are almost identical to those seen in heart disease; (8) elevated blood enzymes—usually seen in heart and liver disease, here the increase is due to muscle breakdown in training; (9) enlarged heart on x-ray.

If all these abnormalities are normal, what about sudden death in athletes?

Wherever adequate investigation has been done, sudden death in athletes has been found to be due to some underlying disease not caused by the sport. The only life-threatening danger to healthy athletes is heat stroke. Severe prolonged exertion in hot, humid weather can kill the unacclimated dehydrated athlete.

Is the athlete at hazard if he gives up his sport?

Theoretically, the ex-athlete simply detrains. After a period of time, he joins his non-playing friends in their state of fitness, or cardiac thrust and cardiac output. In actuality, the athlete who stops his sport tends to continue eating at the same rate and therefore gains an excessive amount of weight. Some cardiologists speculate that this results in a fatty heart.

A philosopher might take an even more pessimistic view. There is no greater privilege than the wholeness of the completely trained and conditioned athlete. The abuse of that privilege must have profound effects not only on his heart but on his mind and soul as well.

Some 30 years ago, I collapsed after a flu shot and an electrocardiogram was done. It was read as abnormal. There were odd-looking T-waves and a blockage of the electrical conduction through the heart. The cardiologist who knew me as a former distance runner did not get excited. He suggested, however, that I best conceal it when I came up for my Navy physical, or I would sit out the war. His colleagues, he intimated, would not be so understanding.

Some 10 years later, I made the mistake of mentioning the EKG during an insurance exam. More EKGs were done. The weird electrical events had, if anything, gotten weirder. They also tended to change from one test to another, which alarmed the insurance people even more. The upshot was that I was offered a policy with the proviso that I pay a double premium.

When I called a medical examiner with a rival company and told him a friend of mine was paying this double premium because of his odd EKG, the examiner assured me his competitors were quite right in imposing the penalty. "Those people," he said, "tend to drop dead."

Yet at that I was racing miles and marathons and running 30-40 miles a week. I'd never felt better in my life. Which is why now I advise every athlete to regard the electrocardiograph machine as a deadly weapon in the hands of those who do not know that fitness and training and inheritance can produce a normal "abnormal" reading.

If the aim of the medical profession is to stop the average American from exercising, it couldn't have done a better job. It is not enough that weather and work and family conspire to make physical fitness as difficult a goal as the peak of Everest. Now the doctors are insisting that before you embark on such an expedition you should not only have a complete physical but an exercise stress test as well.

You know, of course, that a complete physical is not going to turn up anything that your spouse has not already itemized—the stomach, your hips, the double chin. And you know that the recommendations on smoking, drinking and eating will be no different from those already suggested by your mother-in-law. You already know the doctor's verdict: "Good health; lousy shape." So you could talk yourself out of the physical.

But what about the stress test with EKGs and all those sophisticated instruments? Isn't that a logical requirement?

You should know that some experts think the exercise stress test is a high restrictive and expensive and probably unnecessary precaution (Dr. Gordon Cumming, Canadian cardiologist). And others judge it to be of no great value even in the diagnosis of coronary disease (Dr. Stephen Epstein, National Heart Institute). Further, when given without a warmup to presumably healthy people, 70% abnormal results were obtained (Dr. Albert Kattus, UCLA). And in apparently normal women, ages 40-60, almost half had abnormal stress test (Dr. Cumming). If this isn't enough to raise doubts, we should note that European physiologists suggest that much of what we call abnormal is simply excess nervous tone.

Still, as the doctors contend, we do need something to help us prescribe the intensity, frequency and duration of our exercise periods. Fortunately, that something is built into every one of us. Its discoverer, Swedish professor Gunnar Borg, calls it, "perceived exertion." Whatever its name, perceived exertion is the ability to digest all the information coming from the exercising body, the muscles, nerves, heart, lungs, kidneys and everything else, and translate that information into an estimate of physical exertion. What we are doing physiologically, Borg claims, registers quite accurately on a psychological index (rating of perceived exertion).

What this means is we don't need all this electronic wizardry to tell us how hard and how long and how often to exercise. We simply set our Borg scale at "very light" to "fairly light" and start in. If we keep within those bounds, move at a pace at which we can converse with a companion, go at a speed that causes neither chest pain nor excessive fatigue, we are better off than with a treadmill-tested prescription.

Don't forget that laboratory tests are just that: performed at 70 degrees temperature and 40% humidity with no wind. Changing meteorological conditions, proximity to meals, presence of tension or excitement all change the demands on our cardiopulmonary and muscular systems. The machine back in the lab has no answer for this. The body has. Perceived exertion accepts those variables and thousands more, inserts them into our whole body computer and comes up with the answer— the proper pace.

The animal and athlete have always operated this way. The animal especially. No horse ever ran himself to death without a jockey on his back. And no horse would make it to the 7:14 in the morning if he didn't feel just right doing it. Dependence on machines and devices eventually deprives us of the functions— intuition, instinct, body wisdom—for which they are substitutes. It is a major error to use instruments and gadgets as replacements for the natural powers of the whole man moving through and reacting with his environment.

The whole man not only perceives exertion, he perceives exasperation. He not only registers breathing and pulse, cardiac index and muscle lactic acid, oxygen uptake and core temperature; he records anxiety and hostility, anger and fear, guilt and frustration.

It is there that coronaries are bred.

In the 14th century, Tibetan physicians gave up on surgery. Disease, they said, is caused by demons, enviroment, behavior and foods. But mostly one's health is dependent on having a good karma—a combination of a good life style and the expression of the real self in the sum total of thoughts, words and deeds. A bad karma causes illness.

No better description exists for the cause of the 20th century plague, coronary artery disease: the demons of frustration, anger, guilt and failure; an environment of intolerable stress; the behavior of repression, avoidance and denial; a diet to satisfy the emotions. All these bring with them bad karma and breakdown of essential body functions. Disaster must occur sooner or later.

If you have had a heart attack, it may indeed be a blessing in disguise. The chances are the pre-heart attack you was living a destructive, dysrhythmic life, out of synch with the real you that was trying to develop. The odds are great that you were overweight, underexercised and functioning at about 20% of your physical, mental and spiritual capacity. You had, in effect, a bad karma.

Now is the time for you to make a fresh start. First, analyze and eliminate those inner tensions and conflicts that previously complicated your life. Start to develop your real potential. To live at the top of your powers, you must reach the best physical fitness possible for you. This will require a good conditioning program on a daily basis. Your doctor can counsel you on when you can start and on the kind of exercises suitable to your present situation.

Your doctor can tell you about aerobic exercises. He can explain that they stimulate your heart and lungs to increase their function to meet your muscles' demands for more oxygen. He can point out that this is a pay-as-you-go system which takes in whatever oxygen is needed for the task—tasks such as golfing, swimming, jogging, cycling, rope skipping and the rest of those low-pressure endurance activities.

The doctor can tell you about the exercises, but you have to pick the one that goes with your karma—one for which you are physically and psychologically equipped.

This exercise will give you a new and truer image of yourself. It will also give you a fresh understanding of your strengths and weaknesses, and with it a new attitude towards things that would dilute your efforts and change that good feeling you are getting. Problems with smoking, drinking and diet will disappear of their own weight.

Eventually, you will be in much better condition than you were before your heart attack, but that's not all. Your exercise periods will provide time for the examination of the life-style that preceded this illness, to rearrange your priorities, to discover yourself.

Your heart attack could be life-promoting instead of life-threatening. It's all in how you handle it. And what your karma is.

By the age of 50, wrote Camus, a man has the face he deserves. And despite my long nose, overbite and receding chin, I accept that judgment. My face says a great deal about who I am and what I'm doing about it. But it is not my face that tells me I am master of my fate and captain of my soul. It is my pulse.

At any age, a person has the pulse he or she deserves. I regard my heart rate as my own responsibility. Like my nose and my overbite, there are limits to its perfection. But like my face, the obstacles to that perfection are not my genes but the seven capital sins.

The pulse tells me three different things about my body and its capabilities. This information comes from three different aspects of the pulse: (1) the resting pulse rate; (2) the exercise pulse rate; (3) the post-exercise pulse rate.

The resting pulse rate tells me whether or not I am in an inner harmony, in equilibrium with my various body systems. For me, this is achieved when my pulse rate is 48. But for each individual, it is different. For some athletes in training, it can be quite slow. Tennis player Bjorn Borg amazed an examining physician when his heart rate was recorded at 38 beats per minute. This was also the resting rate of Roger Bannister when he broke the four-minute mile barrier.

On the other hand, Jim Ryun's basal pulse when he ran the mile almost nine seconds faster than Bannister was 72. And many Olympic runners have resting pulse rates in that range. A study of 202 Olympians showed that sprinters have average resting rates of 65, middle distance runners 63, long distance runners 61 and marathon runners 58. This last figure was also the one reported for Clarence DeMar, one of the greatest marathoners of all time.

The resting pulse, therefore, simply tells me about my overall fitness. The exercise and post-exercise pulse tell me about my ability to perform and whether at this particular time I can perform up to my maximum.

The exercise pulse is the basis of all ergometry—which is a word that comes from two Greek words, *ergon* meaning work and *metron* meaning measure. The best index of the ability to do work, in my case distance running, is to measure my maximum oxygen uptake. This in turn is determined by my cardiac output or the blood my heart can deliver each minute. That output is simply the number of heart beats per minute times the stroke volume or amount of blood ejected with each beat.

Training increases my stroke volume. Through training, my heart has become capable of delivering five ounces a beat instead of two ounces. Therefore, at a given amount of work, my heart rate might be half of yours. Superstars like Ryun and Bannister are known to be able to put out eight ounces per thrust. And there, beat by beat, is the difference between the men and the boys. I train with a runner who has done 4:06 for the mile. At the same rate of speed, my heart rate is 140, his is 96.

The post-exercise heart rate is yet another indicator which can be used to give me control over my running capabilities. The time the pulse rate takes to come back to normal is the most sensitive index of over- or under-training. This test tells me whether I can take my innate ability (registered by the maximum oxygen uptake) and utilize it to its fullest extent. The post-exercise pulse is the one that really counts.

The reason for this is simple. Like all runners, my hazard is overtraining. Thirty miles a week automatically gets me into inner harmony and brings me to my maximum oxygen uptake. When I add races every week, however, I run the risk of going beyond this fitness, getting into staleness. Keeping a record of the post-exercise pulse is the best way to avoid this. It keeps me in control of my running and my life.

Twelve

Diet and Drugs

When Bob Kiputh was turning out those powerful swimming teams at Yale, he would have nothing to do with vitamins or special foods. His diet was simple. The Breakfast of Champions was a long workout for stamina; the Lunch of Champions was a grueling session for strength, and the Supper of Champions was an exhausting practice for speed. Hard work gives speed, strength and stamina, said Kiputh. Forget about vitamins and latest food fads. They just distract the swimmer from the business at hand.

Thirty years, a hundred food fads and thousands of dietary investigations later, Kiputh's judgment still looks good. Most nutritionists now believe that vitamins and minerals given over and above those in a good mixed diet have no effect on athletic performance. The old Basic Four (milk, fruit-vegetable, meat and bread) give us all we need.

What we need has been established by the Nutrition Board of the National Academy of Science and is known as RDA (Recommended Daily Allowances). These RDAs are, if anything, more liberal than stringent. Certain experiments have shown that any increase over these requirements does nothing for athletic achievement. This was proven for the protein re-

quirement in a study done at the Marine officers school at
Quantico. More red meat, it seems, failed to light any fire under
the Marines. Similarly, the Air Force found vitamin C to be a
washout when given to a large group of exercising officers at
Maxwell Field.

So goes report after report. "There is no evidence," writes
Dr. E. R. Buskirk of Penn State, "that superior performance results from taking more of a single nutrient than required."

Despite the negative evidence, athletes and coaches along
with the general public continue to look for the super diet. Investigations of lockers will turn up such items as queen-bee ex-
tract, seaweed cakes, wheat germ oil, sunflower seeds and
paperbacks on the latest in macrobiotic diets.

Sound physiology as far as food in concerned is ridicu-
lously easy. A couple of programs on the Basic Four on Sesame
Street could make dieticians out of pre-schoolers. But unfortunately, Americans tend to read directions on everything from a
TV set to their own bodies only when things go wrong.

No wonder Dr. Allan Ryan at the University of Wisconsin
found a majority of varsity swimmers, basketball players and
hockey players had diets deficient in RDAs for vitamins A,
C and calcium. Diet to the college athlete is missing breakfast
(that bed is too sweet in the morning), avoiding green and yellow vegetables (why change habits of a lifetime?), cutting down
on milk (in favor of coffee, Coke, beer).

We have already seen that amounts over the RDAs do not
influence an athlete's output. Can we conclude from the Ryan
study that even the RDA amounts may be unnecessary? If the
average college athlete is on a diet lacking the established essentials and yet is by stopwatch, tape measure, blood tests, cardio-
grams and lung capacity tests, superior in fitness to 99% of the
population, what can we say about vitamins? Health foods?
Organic vegetables?

"That's cool, too," or "Whatever turns you on," seem the
most appropriate. The battle, you see, is elsewhere. About 30
years ago at Yale, there was a coach named Kiputh who had a
very simple diet. You begin the morning with. . .

At 5'10" and 143 pounds, I have been described as gaunt, hungry and even cadaveric. My appearance alarms my family and relatives. I am offered extra feedings and double portions to correct my malnutrition, and given turtleneck sweaters to conceal how scrawny I am. But the truth is that I am seven pounds heavier than I was when I was a runner in college, and have triple the percent body fat I had when I was 21. The truth is that, along with millions of Americans, I am fat.

How fat is fat? Pick up your high school or college yearbook and take a look at yourself. If you were an athlete, either officially or unofficially, you will see yourself at ideal body weight and a normal percent of body fat. Otherwise, even then you may have gotten into areas of body fat which the most permissive of physiologists consider abnormal.

What happens next, we all know. As soon as sports end, as soon as we come out of training, as soon as play ends, just as soon does fat start taking over our bodies. When fun and games are replaced by work and marriage and living happily ever after, when we become domesticated and civilized, then and only then do we lose control of our bodies and what they were made to be.

Within a year, we gain the first pound. A few more and the waistline begins to go. In less than 10, the chin gets chubby. Those of us who were athletes go from looking lean and fit to looking "healthy," a sure sign we are 10 or more pounds over the limit. And when later we are called "prosperous," we know that the overweight tally is up to 20. The term "portly" which comes next simply means disaster. We may have financial assets in six figures, but physically we are into deficit financing.

The struggle against this slowly advancing glacier of lard begins before we attain our majority. It never ends. In this war against fat, you have to be a career man. There is no place for 90-day wonders or weekend warriors, no place for crash diets and two-days-a-week exercise. You must begin as a youthful athlete and end as one. You must know that any pound you gain after the age of 21 is neither bone nor muscle. It has to be fat.

The ease with which that fat can be deposited has always alarmed the ordinary citizen. Now it is beginning to alarm the scientists. One reason this gain occurs so readily is that we need more rather than less exercise as we grow older. Dr. Ralph Nelson of the Mayo Clinic has shown that a man who weighs 154 pounds at age 30, and thereafter maintains a constant level of activity on the same caloric intake, will weigh over 200 pounds when he reaches 60. In order to stay the same weight on the same exercise, he must reduce his intake by 11%.

The people who devise those innumerable diets we see month after month in the magazines and newspapers think that reducing the intake is the logical way to approach this matter. They have forgotten that man is the only animal that eats when he is not hungry. So diets do not work—unless man becomes more of an animal, unless he becomes engaged in a daily struggle for survival, either real or simulated.

We know this from watching societies where this communities like those of Vilcabamba in Ecuador, Hunza in Pakistan and Abkhazia in Russo-Georgia, where people work hard and long hours until they are 80, 90 and 100 or more, and where the average daily caloric intake is well under 2000 calories.

What happens there is what happens to the animal in the wild. A man eats only when he is hungry and then only to cover the caloric requirements of his physical activity. So the diet which goes unobserved when the living is easy becomes unnecessary when the living gets hard and difficult and worth the effort.

How fat is fat? Just so much as it takes to alter our image, to blur our structure and blunt our function.

For medical discoveries, nothing beats a prepared mind and a long-suffering patient. Dr. Isadore Snapper found this out during a stay as professor of medicine at the Peking Medical School. His acute observations on otherwise superbly healthy patients who bore their illness with unwavering endurance resulted in a medical classic, *Chinese Lessons to Western Medicine*.

It seems only a matter of time until we see a similar volume based on a study of the diseases of another group of otherwise finely conditioned patients who refuse to give in to their ailments—the athletes. It could be called *Sport's Subtle Sermons for Stumped Specialists*.

The first two chapters may already have been written. First, there's Tom Bache and "The Case of the Million Dollar Knees and the 15 Dollar Shoes." Then there's Gary Berthiaume's "Case of Competition Colic." Bache, is the ex-Marine distance runner who suffered through two years of agony with knee pains. Perhaps his knees weren't worth a million dollars, but the medical talent that was treating them was. And during all that time, his feet were entrusted to the care of a pair of $15 shoes. It was only after two years of suffering, pills, shots and therapy of all sorts that Tom Bache put some arches in his shoes and cured his knees.

Gary Berthiaume has a different problem. Every time he entered a long, tough race he came down with severe stomach pain. Sometimes he would have diarrhea and blood as well. When not running hard and at all other times he had little or no trouble. He sought help from the experts, had x-rays and tests. Nothing abnormal was found. The diagnosis: too much stress during the race and too much nervousness anticipating it.

Berthiaume's response was typical. First, he kept running regardless of the pain. Then he rejected the diagnosis. He knew other men were running as hard without symptoms. And as for being nervous, his attitude was the same as a former surgical giant who, when told that a patient's problem might be psychological because he was so nervous, responded, "Nervous? Of course he's nervous. The question is what else is wrong with him?"

That was Berthiaume's question. Stress obviously played a part. He only developed symptoms after a hard run. But he was peculiarly susceptible to these abdominal complaints, and no one knew why. Investigation of the food was the obvious procedure after the x-rays and other tests were normal. He had no known allergies, and even varying his pre-race meal didn't help. He continued to experience pain severe enough to double him up soon after the race was over.

He finally reduced his pre-race feeding to bread and milk, but he still had trouble. There, as it turned out, lay the answer.

Unknown to Berthiaume and to many who were treating him, a man can be done in by the two most innocent items on his diet, bread and milk—the "staff of life" and the "perfect food for young mammals." Many men it appears cannot live by bread at all, much less alone. And milk after the second decade of life is something most Greek Cypriots, Arabs, Ashkenazi Jews and American Negroes should shun. These people from traditional non-milking areas (and this includes among others the Bantus, Chinese, Thais, Greenland Eskimoes and Peruvian Indians) can have bloating, gas and stomach pains, along with loud noises, after even the small amounts of milk used in cooking.

According to Dr. Theodore Bayless of Johns Hopkins, an expert in this problem, only about 8% of people of Western European extraction have this problem with milk, which is based on a deficiency of lactase (the enzyme that digests lactose, the milk sugar).

Gary Berthiaume was not in that 8%. He could tolerate milk. Bread, or more specifically, gluten (protein found in all grains except corn and rice), was his difficulty. In its full-blown state, the inability to handle gluten is called "sprue" after the Dutch word *sprouw,* meaning chronic diarrhea.

It now appears that some of us may have sprue. Most don't, but many, when placed under stress, can become symptomatic. When the rat race pushes us too fast, or too far, our bowels will let us know. Gluten is always there in our diet, in the bread and baked goods, in the cereals and cereal products, and hidden in soups and gravies, ice cream, wheat germ, mayonnaise and even beer and ale. You can't eat a thing without reading the label.

We should not be surprised that milk and toast, considered the perfect foods for any stomach disorder, have been shown to be the major causes of most of humanity's intestinal malfunctions. Long ago, Dr. Richard Cabot predicted that of all the things the medical profession had done the most embarrassing would be the diets they prescribed for their patients. It took Gary Berthiaume and his competition colic to prove he was right.

The fuel content of an ordinary 150-pound human being is approximately 166,200 calories—1200 in carbohydrate, 25,000 in protein and 140,000 in fat. Yet this 150-pounder, fortified by extra calories at breakfast, must have a coffee break two to three hours later or get the vapours.

Why? The answer is low blood sugar. Most of us suffer from it because we eat the wrong breakfast—or, if you go along with veteran marathoner Aldo Scandurra, from eating breakfast at all.

"When I get up the day of the Boston marathon," Scandurra once told me, "I don't eat at all. I take a large glass of hot water, have a bowel movement, and I'm ready for that race at noon." And what about energy for that long 26 miles? "I have enough already stored up," he replied. "There's no sense upsetting my system with more."

Scandurra is physiologically correct. In the fasting person, the blood sugar stays in a straight line well within the normal range. Only after a meal does it rise, thereby calling for an outpouring of insulin (a hormone of energy storage). When the insulin accomplishes this task, the sugar level drops and you usually know it.

How? Well, you feel as if you need a coffee break. More specifically, that could range from fatigue and yawning or actual drowsiness on the one hand, or a feeling of jitteryness or a light sweat on the other.

The treatment is usually coffee and a Danish. Other therapies include all those quick-energy foods and candies and drinks we see advertised in the press and on TV. The effect is almost immediate. Zing goes the blood sugar—back up and even past normal. This again calls on the insulin to deposit the extra calories. And thus we go on and on depositing high-octane fuel in an already full tank, depositing fat on top of fat when all we had to do was call on the energy we already had stored for use.

Can this be done? Can low blood sugar be cured without diet or treated without jelly sandwiches, candy bars and fruit juice? Can we raise our blood sugar any time we want to?

Why not? Children and athletes do. What do grammar school students do at 10:30 in the morning when they get the same feeling that sends grown men and housewives to the kitchen or the snack bar? They have recess. They get out and raise a sweat, and in the process elevate their blood sugar. They then come back to the classroom renewed and intelligent, becoming more docile, more teachable. The transformation is a physiological one.

And what of the athlete? He has the same meal. He has been advised to have a relatively high carbohydrate meal before his event. If nothing else, it is more easily digested. Then he waits the two to three hours. Insulin, the hormone of energy storage, is doing its work. His blood sugar starts down. He begins to yawn (spectators mistakenly marvel at how casually he seems to be taking the race), or gets into a light, clammy perspiration. Does he then look around for food, something to raise his blood sugar? Of course not. He knows he is ready to release this power he has crammed into his muscles and liver. This is what these feelings mean to an athlete.

So he does the only appropriate thing, the natural thing for the human animal. He goes into physical action. That action, for reasons we did not know until recently, has to be intense enough to cause sweating and prolonged enough to call on what has been described as that "miraculous refreshment and renewal of vigor"—the second wind.

We now read that there is a good scientific reason for all of this. The pancreas which produces insulin, a hormone of energy storage, also produces glucagon, a hormone of energy release.

Further, when the athlete exercises he stimulates the production of glucagon, with the result that all the fuel he has stashed away in the last meal—and the past week and past year, if necessary—begins to pour out into the blood. *Voila*, the blood sugar rises.

There is a time, the Bible says, for everything. There is a time for low blood sugar. There is a time for high blood sugar. There is time for insulin. There is a time for glucagon. There is a time for meat, a time for bread, and a time for nothing at all. The problem is finding the right time.

Has the energy crisis of the athlete been solved? Is there a "best" diet for athletic performance and endurance? An eat-program that will bring the athlete to a peak effort Saturday after Saturday? An optimal pre-event meal?

The answer to all of these questions, if we can believe research already done and extrapolate work now in progress, is a clear, firm, unhesitating "yes."

The athlete does have a diet available to him which can improve his endurance capacity as much as 100%, his maximum performance 5-10%. He can eat a prescribed pre-event meal which will insure him the best and quickest use of the energy it contains. And he has a quantity of effective quick-energy drinks he can use freely during the contest to maintain his stamina.

The "super-compensation diet" was discovered by Swedish physiologist Eric Hultman. Its aim is to get maximum storage of sugar in the body as muscle glycogen. It is this glycogen which is the essential source of energy for the muscle during strenuous exercise.

Using cross-country skiers as subjects, Hultman found that by manipulating diets and training schedules he could give the athletes super-normal stores of this readily available energy substance. Eventually he came up with a program incorporating three fundamental steps:

1. A prolonged exhausting workout which depleted the stores of glycogen in the muscles.

2. Three days of low carbohydrate intake. It made very

little difference whether the athlete took a high-protein diet, high-fat diet or starved himself. What was required was abstinence from carbohydrates in any quantity.

3. Three days of high carbohydrate intake. The athlete was given large amounts of cereals, bread, fruits, vegetables, honey, jelly, etc. This caused the supercompensation and deposition of glycogen stores up to twice or three times normal.

Control subjects who were given a high-protein diet or a balanced diet after the exhausting workout failed to show this rise. When exercised on bicycle ergometers, those on the high protein diet had a maximum work time of 57 minutes, those on the balanced diet had a MWT of 114 minutes and those on the super-sugar diet lasted 167 minutes.

This conclusive laboratory demonstration was confirmed in field trials on runners by another Swede, Bengt Saltin. In a 30-kilometer race, runners on the high-carbohydrate regimen had a mean time of 135 minutes versus 143 while on the balanced diet.

The answer to endurance and performance, then, is to stockpile sugar in the form of glycogen, and to do this you must first drain your muscles of this glycogen and then cause an overshoot by stoking up on high-carbohydrate foods. Protein, the traditional food for strength and vigor, is of little use. Glycogen, Hultman learned, is synthesized 10 times faster from sugar than protein.

The optimal pre-event meal is now obvious. It must be more of the same: easily-digested high-carbohydrate foods that the athlete knows agree with his stomach and bowels, taken early enough to be in the muscles as glycogen when the gun goes off. Forget the beefsteak. It won't help.

The way I see it, Hultman has come up with something we knew from the earliest times. Our caveman ancestors, when successful in the hunt, would have some days of gorging on protein and fat corresponding to the first three days of Hultman's schedule. Then he would like as not have an exhausting unsuccessful hunt. Now reduced to roots and herbs, one would expect him to lose strength and endurance, perhaps perish. But he

is almost miraculously restored by this seemingly inadequate diet and again has a successful hunt.

If it is next year, not this, that you plan to exercise at the "Y," start on the low-cholesterol diet, quit smoking, see a relaxed you at work and your own man at home, you may join the hundreds of thousands of Americans who risk a heart attack or stroke this year.

The game, however, is not entirely up. There is chance that procrastination may be safe, if you follow the latest advice on the latest wonder drug—"an aspirin a day keeps the doctor away."

Aspirin, say the experts on blood clotting, can prevent the platelets-clots that form in the arteries of our brain and heart and cause heart attacks and strokes. The platelets are microscopic particles in the blood which become very sticky under certain circumstances and aggregate into crowds called clots. Aspirin reduces this adhesiveness and keeps these vagrant platelets from loitering around and causing trouble.

This startling information may be of no benefit to those in whom aspirin causes asthma or skin rashes or even stomach hemorrhages, but the rest of us may now have a lifetime until we reorder the priorities of our life.

An aspirin a day seems a lot more scientific than an apple, although it doesn't have the biblical ring of the forbidden fruit and doesn't make us think of the Song of Solomon, or the 11th labor of Hercules. The apple had gone the way of the buggy whip, wood-burning stoves and homemade bread. It has been replaced by a chemical. Aspirin, the product of the technological age, has become the drug for the diseases of that technological age.

Antibiotics, you see, have killed the old killers and left the field to the degenerative diseases, heart attacks and strokes. The thrust of medicine has turned from cure to prevention—how best to prevent heart attacks, how best to forestall the stroke.

Our friends, the scientists, have not replaced the known preventitives—diet, exercise, avoiding tension, stopping smoking. All these measures prevent the hardening of the arteries that predeces these episodes. But the aspirin, which has no effect on this narrowing of the blood vessels, can prevent the small clots that finally clog them.

This property of aspirin has been suspected for some time but never taken seriously. Back in 1956, Dr. L. L. Craven reported that he had given 8000 of his patients aspirin in two-tablets-a-day doses for a period of 10 years without observing a heart attack or a stroke. But it wasn't until three or four years ago that researchers came up with definite evidence that aspirin was indeed effective in preventing arterial clots.

They are also finding other things that affect the stickiness of platelets. Some are obvious. Emotional stress, smoking, and a diet rich in egg yolk and butter-fat increases this stickiness. A five-mile walk and other types of endurance exercise tends to keep the platelets apart.

All of this has led one researcher, Dr. Lee Wood of the City of Hope Medical Center in California, to write, "I suggest that men over the age of 20 and women over the age of 40 should take one aspirin tablet a day on a chronic long-term basis." This routine, says Wood, would lessen the incidence and severity of arterial clotting diseases. In additional support of this view, he points to the low incidence of heart attacks in patients with rheumatoid arthritis, patients who usually take aspirin on a daily basis.

We are moving toward an exciting and unexpected change in our life-styles, a change brought about in the coming decades by our leisure activities and sports and athletics. We are moving toward a climate that will breed another more physical, and because of that, more intellectual and more spiritual man.

But now in mid-passage between the flabby American and the paragon he will become, we need acetylsalicyclic acid in small doses to save us. While we are marking time, unwilling or unable to make the committment to a fitness program, the best advice may be one that we used to joke about: "Take two aspirin and call me in the morning."

What's in a name? The overweight matron calls them "diet pills." The cross-country bus driver calls them "bennies." To the cramming student, they are "pep pills." The addicts call them "uppers." Olympic physicians use the term "ergogenic aids." To *Sports Illustrated*'s Bil Gilbert, they are simply drugs.

These names and uses of the amphetamines suggest that they are at once legal and illegal, helpful and harmful, addictive and non-addictive, even moral and immoral. The time has come, according to Gilbert, and other spokesmen for the sports world, to take a stand on the use of these substances in athletics. Unfortunately, the debate over the use of drugs in athletics suffers from the same defect as the debate over the use of drugs by the general public. Lack of information.

The effect of amphetamines on performance is an area where conjecture and myth have been substituted for facts. What reports we do have suggest that amphetamines are bad news in complicated problem-solving sports like football. Not only do subjects lose the ability to solve the problems, but like the three-martini wizards they think they are doing a fine job. Misjudging performance is a common characteristic of athletes under the influence of these drugs. Experiments with swimmers showed that to a man they felt they swam faster with the pills, but their times were either the same or slower than the control runs.

This is a major theme of MIT professor Jerome Letwin, who says that any skill that can be recorded, measured or quantified deteriorates under the drugs even though the user thinks he has surpassed his usual performance. Reasons for this are easily seen with pot and other hallucinogens. But why should it happen with a stimulant like amphetamine? What may happen is that the immediate psychological lift of the drug is accompanied by use of body energy, while still at rest. In this way, the athlete loses some of his reserve energy.

The danger is that he may exceed his safety limit as did the English cyclist Tony Simpson. Simpson, under the influence of amphetamines, collapsed and died while climbing a 6000-foot mountain during the 1967 Tour of France. Unfortunately, he may not be the last of the bicyclists to succumb to drugs. The professional cyclist faced with the grueling Tour of France, a 21-day 3000-mile ride worth $200,000 to the winner, is willing to take chances. Simpson, after all, was careless. It was 90 degrees and he was using "speed," the most dangerous of all amphetamines.

Jacques Anquetil, a five-time winner of the Tour, is an admitted amphetamine user. Anquetil has said, "I dope myself. Everyone dopes himself. Those who claim they don't are liars."

In such instances, the pep pill is a whip administered to a tired horse. Its primary effect is on the psyche, to increase ambition and dull pain. But it cannot increase the total available energy. And the normal instincts of survival may be dulled, with ensuing collapse—perhaps with fatal outcome.

Gilbert's extensive investigation of the problem, however, has led him to conclude that "the cold objective point is that drugs do not kill or corrupt enough athletes to constitute anything but a very minor health problem." He is against drugs because they remove the "drama and mystery" by fixing the outcome.

Some, including Dutch physician E. J. Ariens, are willing to accept this possibility by allowing free use of drugs as long as they are prescribed by a licensed doctor. This may be a startling approach to many of us, but this permissive attitude is growing rapidly among many researchers working with drugs—mostly with marijuana.

Any long-term settlement of the drug situation must take into account this presumptive evidence of the widespread, nonchalant use of "grass" by the younger generation. They have come to a consensus about "soft" drugs. Marijuana may be illegal, they are saying, but it is no worse than alcohol or even (according to some) coffee and cigarettes. On the other hand, "hard" drugs are for freaks and losers.

My guess is that athletes will continue to find the greatest "ergogenic aid" is hard work and training.

It comes as no news to us working stiffs that caffeine is being touted as the best drug to aid athletic performance. The *New York Times* quoted Dr. David James, a chemist in Switzerland and a former world class sprinter, as the source of this information. According to James, the use of caffeine laced with a little niacinamide—one of the B-complex vitamins— was widespread among European athletes.

James studied 30 Swiss athletes and discovered what every coffee drinker knows: caffeine delayed fatigue and increased motor activity. His work confirmed that of the Cleveland Clinic's Robert Mercer. Mercer told an Ohio State symposium on sports, "If your athlete feels tired or nervous and feels the need for aid to increase his efficiency, I suggest that you give him a cup of coffee." All other drugs thought to increase strength or ability, he said, were either risky or useless, or both.

My own impression, as someone with a Ph.D. in coffee, is that we've been had. All those reams of stories we've been reading about athletes winning because of drugs are hogwash. The coffee drinker, as every coffee drinker knows, is a loser trying to be a winner and never quite making it.

Coffee has, of course, a beneficial effect on my performance, just as I suppose it has on yours. Like millions of Americans, we are unable to face the day without it, incapable of getting up without the aroma of percolating coffee to pry us from sleep's comforting oblivion. Without coffee, living would not be worthwhile or even possible.

The net effect, however, is only an approximation of the morning energy enjoyed by that small but hated minority who rise with a song on their lips to greet the rosy-fingered dawn. Coffee or no, we cannot hope to equal the smiling good health of those noisy peasants who are already full of activity because the morning's at seven and the lark's on the wing and God's in His heaven. They are the early-to-bed, early-to-rise people who need no stimulants to get them underway. They awake with all systems "go." For them, the crack of day has the same effect as a starter's pistol. They are the medal winners, the champions.

For the rest of us dullards (and Swiss athletes), coffee is

the help Drs. James and Mercer say it is. But that help will never bring us to our full potential. We are hooked and wander through the day from one coffee break to another. If we could shake the habit, we would be the better for it. We could join those who live in the world without coffee and tea and colas, the world where champions live.

Why not give up coffee? We have, after all, nothing to lose but our chains. I went that route once. It took five miserable days and the non-coffee world was all they said it was. It was a California-like world where there are no seasons, just one beautiful day after another. It lacked, however, the exhilaration of spring, the gloom of a wet November, the excitement of winter, the weariness of August. It lacked the moods and the coffee to go with them. On the sixth day, I came back.

Thirteen

Breaths and Burps

Is the "second-wind" a myth? Is it a romantic term left over from the days when every hero had a stout heart, a clean conscience—and a second-wind?

In 1915, the great physiologist Walter Cannon called the second wind, "an almost miraculous refreshment and renewal of vigor."

Yet most physiologists today seem to doubt its existence. And those who mention it do so only to disparage it. "It has been demonstrated," writes English exercise expert Vaughan Thomas, "that the second-wind has no effect on performance."

Even if you translate second-wind into "warmup" you will find that researchers are split down the middle on whether a warmup does the athlete any good. In their *Scientific Basis of Athletic Conditioning*, Jensen and Fisher report eight "yeas" and seven "nays" for the warmup idea, which are the usual statistics pollsters obtain in issues where emotions, not facts, are at issue.

But I'm here to state that the second-wind does exist. I have experienced and continue to experience almost daily that "miraculous refreshment"—that point when the runner's transmission slips into high gear and running suddenly becomes rhythmic and effortless.

If you start a training run at a slow speed, keeping well within yourself, at about six minutes this feeling of being the complete runner will steal over you and possess you. The only external sign for me is a warm, pleasant sweat. Inside is euphoria and confidence.

Is this all mental, a form of self-hypnosis? Not if you listen to the psychobiologists. These men, the offspring of a marriage between psychology and exercise physiology, started with the idea that what was important was not "what the individual was doing" but rather "what he *thinks* he is doing."

"Perceived exertion" (what the runner said he felt) was, they found, directly correlated to what their sophisticated instruments said was happening to the heart and lungs and muscles. The runner's sensations do indeed result from his physiological processes. He is a totality of mind and body reacting totally. If the runner reports a second-wind, a feeling that the running is measurably easier, then the second-wind exists.

Why then have the physiologists failed to demonstrate this phenomenon? Why have they been unable to capture this happening on their graphs and charts? The reason, I suggest, is that they have been looking in the wrong places. The natural habitat of the second-wind is natural man. Primitive man, leaving his cave for the day's hunt, certainly started at an easy lope that allowed the body processes to adjust. He surely sought a pace which would give him the feeling that the chase would be successful.

Unless scientists reconstruct these essentials—the start from rest and a slow pace—experiments to find the second wind and its effects will fail. On the few occasions when these precautions have been observed, the experiment has been successful.

At the Tokyo Olympics, for instance, Japanese researchers recruited the world's outstanding marathoners for such an investigation. Using a treadmill and these previously rested runners, they did indeed demonstrate the physiological changes of the second-wind. The most clearcut results were noted in the case of the great Abebe Bikila.

This two-time Olympic gold medalist got on the treadmill without prior warmup and started running at an easy pace. His heart rate and respiratory rate gradually rose over a period of three minutes, reaching a plateau. And then suddenly, at the three-minute mark (it was later for the less gifted), Bikila had a sharp drop in his pulse and breathing. He also began to sweat and his blood pressure widened. He was in the perfect physiological state for distance running.

It is as simple as that. Easy and natural does it. You have to avoid rush and bustle and pushing and shoving, and put away impatience and force and speed, if you want to find your second-wind.

In autumn, the sound of my belch is heard through the land. Fall is the Camelot of runners. There are races every-where—races run in air turned crisp and invigorating, the perfect temperature for distance running.

But the races also bring tension. In those minutes before the start, I feel threatened. I know I may be beaten. I know I will surely feel pain. And not only my mind knows this, my entire body knows it and acts accordingly. Hence, the belch. That is the way I react when I am in a situation where I am embarrassed, frustrated or apprehensive. The belch is something rarely uttered in anger. It is not the roar of a lion, but the bleat of a sheep.

You might say I was born with this belch. I was certainly born with a dominant vagus nerve which causes spasms of the stomach and excess secretion of acid, especially when under stress. I was also born loosely tied together. Because of this defect in my tissues, my cutoff valve that keeps gas or gastric juice from going back up my esophagus is weak. Put acid and spasm and a weak valve together and there is my belch.

Still, even with these explanations, some think my belch indefensible. To all but the belcher, this noise seems to be produced by conscious effort and therefore is easily suppressed. Physicians regard belchers as air swallowers, put them down as neurotics and the cause of their own problems. No wonder the belcher begins to feel like a pariah, an object of ridicule in society, misunderstood even in his own home (which, incidentally, makes him belch even more).

I have found, however, new support for the argument that I am a product of forces beyond my control. When appeals to consider my faulty heredity fail, when no one will listen to my story of being born with hyperacidity and an incompetent esophageal sphincter, I can now discuss Niko Tinbergen. Tinbergen has credibility. He shared the Nobel Prize for biology in 1972 with Konrad Lorenz and Karl Van Frisch. He earned this award by observing how animals behave in their natural lives in the wild. One of the ways of behavior is displacement movements, which are apparently inappropriate or irrelevant actions performed when the animal cannot discharge some powerful motivation. Such a situation occurs when the fighting drive and the drive to escape are both activated. When faced with this internal discord, the male three-spine stickleback digs a hole. I belch.

An extension of these displacement activities to humans has already been made. Tinbergen gives yawning as an example. And, of course, yawning is a phenomenon prevalent in competitive running. Before important races, many runners yawn constantly. I recall hearing a spectator comment on how relaxed these yawning runners were, when actually it was an indication of the tremendous tension building up inside of them.

Other innate actions like scratching your ear or rearranging your hair are instances of displacement activities, as are certain learned patterns like lighting a cigarette or handling keys. All say the same thing: this particular human animal is in conflict. So the belch I emit as I place my foot just behind the starting line means I dread what is about to happen. I would much rather be somewhere else.

Once the gun sounds, however, resolution occurs. All is now changed. I am now totally mobilized to this new action and the belch, which is really the sound of a man in a dilemma, is gone.

I move to the rhythm of my breathing, gradually settling into my own tempo, neither pursuing nor pursued. The pain comes and is accepted. There are groans alternating with "Oh God!" on the last mile through the hills. But then I can see the finish and I let everything go.

Afterwards, there is peace. It will be hours, perhaps even days before I start belching again.

The "stitch" will never make Disease-of-the-Month or have a foundation named after it. Discovering the cure for the stitch won't mean the Nobel Prize, or an invitation to the White House, or even a line in the medical journals. But it will make a lot of runners happy. And it will silence those malcontents who go around saying, "They can put a man on the moon but they can't cure the stitch."

Oddly enough, it looks as if "they" are about to cure the stitch. The pieces are coming together. The pieces are "backward breathing" and "air trapping," and their antidotes "belly-breathing" and "resistance."

But let's start at the beginning. The stitch is known to be due to diaphragm spasms. This excruciating pain in the lower rib cage and its frequent satellite pain in the shoulder is caused by a charleyhorse of the muscle that divides the chest from the abdomen. The stitch is the diaphragm gone haywire. Man's perfectly designed ventilatory system is being mishandled by its owner.

The most obvious maltreatment is the sudden, prolonged use of the diaphragm in a sedentary individual. The diaphgragm is accustomed to moving 1.5 centimeters 18 times a minute while we are at rest. Maximal effort brings those figures to nearly seven centimeters a breath and a rate of 45 breaths a minute. No wonder the diaphragm complains.

Such demands on an unconditioned muscle explain the stitch that occurs in beginning runners. But what of the veteran runners who still are bedeviled by this spasm? What about accomplished distance runners who still experience this pain from time to time?

These athletes, the scientists suggest, are doing other and more serious things to their diaphragms. They are breathing backward or trapping air, or both. Pulmonary function experts are finding that certain normal people have a tendency for their tiny bronchial tubes to collapse and accumulate air in the lungs. Breathing backward is a much more common phenomenon. When I breathe, my diaphragm should go down and my belly out. A minute's observation will convince most people they are doing quite the opposite. When they breathe in, their bellies go in; when they breathe out, their bellies go out.

When the diaphragm is being stretched by air trapping and further stretched by backward breathing, it is only a matter of time until the runner once more experiences the most dreaded of all racing pains—the stitch.

Knowing these mechanisms, however, we can now move toward a cure. This means no less than a complete re-education of the breathing cycle, the sort of thing you might learn best from a singing teacher rather than a track coach. Maximum breath control is a necessary—you could say vital—part of every singer's schooling. They have to develop the ability to fill every nook and cranny of their lungs before they go into those arias.

Only the correct belly breathing method can do this. At the same time, singers are automatically correcting any tendency to trap air. Singing, which is expelling air against resistance, is as good a way as any to keep these small bronchial tubes from collapsing and retaining air. In fact, any slight resistance to exhalation will do it. Some simple home exercises may do just as well:

1. Learn to use your diaphragm correctly. Lie on the floor with a weight or books on your stomach. As you breathe the books should rise. Keep this up until you breathe this way naturally. It is, after all, the way the body was designed to breathe. One difficulty will be tight stomach muscles. Stretching exercises usually have to be done quite persistently to overcome this difficulty.

2. Make it a habit of breathing out against a slight re-

sistance. An occasional groan to get maximal exhalation is very helpful. Groaning also induces you to contract your stomach muscles when you breathe out. Some very good runners grunt or groan with each breath even in long races. They have apparently found on their own the value of belly-breathing and exhaling against resistance.

Fourteen

Age and Ability

Do athletes live longer than non-athletes? Will winning a letter in school add years to your life? Has early physical competence anything to do with later survival? Do sportsmen, in short, have a greater Longevity Quotient than their spectator classmates?

In a world whose disease is heart disease and whose best remedy may be exercise, such questions have increasing significance. Unfortunately, the answers the scientists come up with are yes, or no, or maybe.

Yes, writes Dr. Curtis Prout, who found that Yale and Harvard oarsmen lived over six years longer than randomly selected classmates.

No, claims Dr. Peter Schnorr, who discovered that 297 Danish champions who attained the age of 50 thereafter lived no longer than the average for the country.

Maybe, asserts Dr. Dale Largey, who studied life spans in "Who Was Who in American Sports" and found that athletes in certain sports—especially track—lived longer than the average.

The waters have been further muddied by Dr. Anthony Polednack, whose study of 6303 Harvard men pointed out that winning a letter might add years to your life—but only if it was in a minor sport. Major athletes according to Polednack, died significantly earlier than non-athletes from coronary heart disease, and perhaps earlier and more often from tumors.

Despite these discrepancies and apparent disagreements, the whole question has, it seems to me, a fairly simple solution. None of the studies shows whether or not the athletes remained athletes. We can assume they didn't. Polls in England, where sports participation runs high, disclosed that only 10% of married men ages 23-30 continued their sports activities. Americans probably have an even worse record.

The question that these researchers are asking is, "Do ex-athletes live longer than non-athletes?" The answer is "Probably not." The differences detected by Drs. Prout, Schnorr, Polednack and Largey are simply the tendency of our population to have different life spans, based on body build. Your carcass, which anthropologist Earnest Hooten said is the best clue to your character, is also the best clue to your allotted life span.

The muscular, aggressive ex-football players are statistically susceptible to cardiovascular disease to just that degree shared by their muscular, aggressive non-athletic counterparts. Onlookers who share the magnificent physical and psychological attributes of crewmen will share in their extended life span. Thin, small-boned people represented in sports by distance runners are genetically programmed to live longer than the general average.

All this may explain our present information, but it leaves still to be answered the question of whether or not an athletic program continuing into middle age has any effect on our longevity. Do athletes live longer than ex-athletes? Can the Longevity Quotient be enhanced by fitness and reduced by a life-style of overindulgence and psychological stress?

The answer to that, I suspect, is "yes." Such a premise is strengthened by the findings of Dr. Ernst van Aaken on the effects of maximal endurance running. Reviewing reports on 1000 members of the Association of Veteran Long Distance Runners between the ages of 40-90 from 29 countries, Dr. van Aaken did not find one case of a heart attack or cancer in five years of observation.

This almost incredible statement is supported by the work of Dr. Thomas Bassler who has found almost absolute immunity to coronary disease in runners actively competing at the marathon distance or training six miles or more per day.

The moral is obvious: Like everyone else, including the wife and kids, your body keeps asking, "Yes, but what have you done for me lately?"

Consider the nine-year old. If anyone has made it in this life, it's the nine-year-old. You could, of course, just say the child. That would put you right with the Lord ("Unless you become as little children, you shall not enter the kingdom of heaven") and the poets like Eliot ("The end of all our exploring will be to arrive where we started, and know the place for the first time").

The child is the answer, and, of those years, I pick the nine-year-old. He is pound for pound the world's best endurance athlete. And he moves with the grace and elegance of the free animal. He has, as German physiologists have discovered, the biggest heart volume for his weight that he will ever have unless he is an Olympic champion. He is therefore the nearest thing to perpetual motion in human form you will ever see. And yet he is capable at other times of the contented lethargy of a lion after a kill.

The nine-year-old can teach us a lot about our bodies. He does nothing, you see, that his body doesn't tell him is in some way good. Consider some of his instinctive reactions: his recess periods, his desire to go barefoot, his aversion to baths.

Take recess for one—those quarter-hours of helter skelter bedlam and hilarity, those 15 minutes of maximum unprogrammed physical activity with the noise level of Kennedy Airport. Where are adults' recesses? Gone, of course. Gone and replaced by low blood sugar and coffee breaks. Now that mid-morning feeling that called us to action, that low blood sugar that told us we were now ready for our best physical effort, is being dieted and medicated and fed out of existence. Only the nine-year-old knows his recess brings him and his blood sugar up to normal until lunch. If we listened to him, the streets would be filled with running, playing people about 10:30 every morning.

For the nine-year-old, playing comes naturally. No Canadian Air Force exercises for him. His preferences come from his total person, not the dictates of social status or medical authorities. If we take to exercise now, we should remember what we liked to do when we were nine, before we began to conform, to do the "right" things, to follow the current craze whether it be jogging, skiing or weight lifting.

Whatever the nine-year-old does, he is in no hurry. His tempo is decided by his body and senses and emotions working in harmony. Ready at times to exploit to the fullest every hour of the day, to use himself to the bone, he also can spend a day in idleness, recognizing all these actions as ends, not means.

Whatever he does, he would prefer to do it in bare feet. Every schoolboy knows shoes to be the enemy. The foot wants no shoe, no more than the body wants to ride in a car. If we must have shoes, let them be the mold of our footprints. Some adults have already discovered that and are making shoes like that footprint.

Some adults may also discover the truth about baths. Why do nine-year-olds who love to swim hate baths? Why do children who won't leave the water in the summertime refuse to get into a tub in the winter? Swimming is good; baths are bad.

It could be simply esthetics. The bathtub is not the finest work of art in the house. But it may be more than that. Baths in the winter lead to chills and chills to colds. Baths also drain energy. Any athlete or nine-year-old knows that. Baths make one relaxed and sleepy, and no one with the world and its wonders in front of him wants to sleep.

So the nine-year-olds do have lessons for us. They are, I suspect, one of those small "pockets of phenomena" which anthropologists like Claude Levi-Strauss are studying to understand other ways of life, other ways of happiness.

"Anthropology," says Levi-Strauss, "invites us to temper our pride and to respect other life styles."

I'll take the life style of the nine-year-old: spontaneous, effortless, innocent and easy, filled with wonder and new things to which he responds totally with his head, his heart, his gut.

Aging is a continuous, linear process. Body time does not bend. It is not relative; it is relentless. Our lives follow an appointed course. We may not go gentle into that good night, but we will go and we will go at a predictable rate. Here and there, some slip through the net—a Picasso, a Granda Moses, an occasional athlete, not a few ballerinas. But they are quirks of nature. For them, the bad genes are absent, as they are in those mountain people living in enclaves like Hunza and Vilcabamba and Abkhazia.

The rest of us echo the Psalmist: "Let me know, O Lord, my end and the number of my days that I may know how frail I am." That's what we want to know: exactly how frail we are, when we peak physically and what is in store for us in the future. What can we expect at one and 20, one and 40, one and 60, one and 80?

Some centuries back, Aristotle suggested that the physical acme occurred between the ages of 30 and 35. The intellectual acme he put later, at the age of 51. Aquinas set the end of youth and the beginning of wisdom at the age of 40. Only then, he thought, could a person become a philosopher. Clemenceau remarked that everything he knew, he had learned after he was 30. There is, you see, a general agreement that aging has merits for the mind, as it does for fine wine.

But testing intelligence and imagination and creativity is a chancy business, and rarely convincing. It is not yet the science that scientists make out. Applied physiology is, on the other hand, at a point where very sophisticated measurements of bodily function can be made quite accurately. With such methods, we should get all the answers we need about when we peak and how fast we age.

Unfortunately, we don't get those answers. We can measure decreases in vital capacity, kidney function, near vision, basal metabolism, sense of taste, cardiac output and more. But we are

not at all sure what those changes mean when it comes to over-all performance of the human body. The question remains as to what the ordinary person can do in a real-life situation when he puts his mind and body into it.

I think we are finally getting some answers. Dr. L. E. Bottinger, a professor of medicine at the Karolinska Hospital in Stockholm, has one answer. Bottiger took the problem out of the laboratories and onto the ski course of Vasa and the running course of Lidingo in Sweden. And in place of the 25 medical students in the usual experiment, he had 7625 skiers and 1911 runners—a cross-section of the population with regard to age, occupation, education, etc. And this was not just a few minutes on the treadmill. The Vasa race extends a distance of 87 kilo-meters (54 miles); Lidingo is a shorter, faster race of 30 kilometers (19 miles).

Bottinger sorted out the Vasa and Lidingo finishers into age groups of five years—starting with the 16-20 sample and ending with 61-65. Taking the mean time of these groups, he made two findings of great interest:

● The best performances (lowest times) were turned in by the 31-35-year-old skiers and the 26-30-year-old runners.

● The times rose from that point practically linearly with age. This decrease in performance came to approximately 6-7% every 10 years.

The younger age of the runners reflects the less demanding nature of the event. Lidingo is more purely physical. Vasa is a super-endurance race where technique and psychological factors play a large role. And here age has the edge.

Taken together, these races tell us more than we ever knew about when a body peaks, and when and how fast its physical working capacity declines. Bottinger's work is a thing of beauty. The size of the sample is awesome, the statistics are beyond question, the experimental situation is unparalleled. But what thrills the reader more is the evidence of the enormous power of the common man—and more particularly the *aging* common man.

Time may be relentless, but Vasa and Lidingo prove that we were not made to be spectators. We are continually capable of doing whatever we did in our prime—a little slower, perhaps, somewhat weaker, surely, but if they wait around long enough we'll finish.

One of the beautiful things about running is that age has no penalties. The runner lives in an eternal present. The passage of time does not alter his daily self-discovery, his struggles and his sufferings, his pains and his pleasures. The decline of his ability does not interfere with the constant interchange between him, his solitude, and the world and everyone around him. And neither of these happenings prevents him from challenging himself to the ultimate limit, putting himself in jeopardy, courting crisis, risking catastrophe.

Because he refuses to look back, the runner remains ageless. That is his secret, that and the fact that his pursuit of running is in obedience to, in Ellen Glasgow's phrase, "a permanent and self-renewing inner compulsion."

In my 50s, I am aware of all this. Like all runners, I live in the present. I am not interested in the way we were. The past is already incorporated in me. There is no use returning to it. I live for the day. Running gives me self-expression, a way of finding out who I am and who I will be. It makes me intimate with pain. I know the feeling of too little oxygen, of too much lactic acid. I have, always within reach, the opportunity to test my absolute barriers, to search out the borders set up by straining muscles and a failing brain.

But what about performance and competition? What about time and place? How does the aging runner handle the stopwatch? How can he feel really competitive during a race? The answers are (1) age-rated performances, and (2) age-group races.

For less than the entry fee to the Boston marathon, you can get a computer printout of your age-rated performances for every standard running distance. With this point scoring, you can compare your results not only with your own achievements from year to year, but with world class (1000 points), or national championship (900), or high school dual meet (600-700) performances.

Age-group racing normally begins at age 40 for older runners (there's a similar program for the very young), with classes split down to five-year increments.

Together, they make age 55 as exciting as 21. They make every race important, and therefore stimulating and absorbing and exhilarating just like mine on one weekend.

The first was the 40-and-over mile. Normally, I would be over my head in the 40-and-over race. Some of these runners arrive at the line with the icing of their 40th birthday cake still on the corners of their mouths. But this time only one really good runner, Joe Bessel, showed up. Bessel won by a hundred yards to polite applause. But the crowd was on its feet and shouting for three of us fighting it out down that last furlong, the longest homestretch I have ever seen.

I just outlasted the other two in 5:19 (840 points) and afterward received my plaque from Ben Jipcho (an 1100-point miler). Now you can say what you will, but there are not too many ways a 55-year-old can equal taking a second place, running the equivalent of a 4:17 mile and getting his prize from one of the world's best milers—especially when Ben Jipcho says "Fantastic . . ." in handing it to you.

The weekend, however, was not over. A five-mile race with 300 entries was the next day. Here, I moved back into the 50-and-over category and my initial appraisal at the starting line disclosed there was no one to worry about. I could concentrate on my form, my time and my point score. Winning the 50-and-over would take care of itself.

So I was in a state of happy agony nearing the finish, knowing I was the winner in my division, when I saw Rod Nichols up ahead. I had always thought of Rod as a very good runner working out his salvation in the 40-and-over group. But I suddenly noticed that Rod was getting quite bald, and it occurred to me that Rod had been around the running scene for a very long time. He began to look more and more like a very competent 50-year-old.

At considerable cost, partially paid for by the panic I felt at this thought, I caught up to him. Easing alongside, I casually gasped, "How old are you, Rod?"

"I'm 75," he replied in a tone just short of exasperation, and then added, "I'm 44."

I relaxed. I didn't have to beat him. When he gets to be 50, I thought as I cruised around the high school track to the finish, I'll be in the 60-and-over.

James Joyce took the 10 years of Homer's *Odyssey* and compressed them into a Dublin day. He looked into the mind and heart and body of the hero Ulysses and created Leopold Bloom, who is everyman. Joyce saw in the Lotus-eaters, Cyclops, the Gift of the Winds, Circe, Hades, the Sirens and even the nymph Calypso those inner and outer events that happen to everyone every day of his life. And then he put all of it into the waking to sleeping of his Irish Jew. It takes 18 hours.

The Boston marathon does it in three. Like all sports, the marathon is a microcosm of life. The marathoner can experience the drama of everyday existence so evident to the artist and poet. For him, all emotions are heightened. Cause and effect are accelerated. Agony and ecstasy become familiar feelings. The journey from Hopkinton to Boston, like the journey from Troy to Ithaca, reveals what happens to man when he faces up to himself and the world around him, and why he succeeds or fails.

Ulysses succeeds not because he is a superior athlete, which he is. He can build a boat and sail it. He can wrestle, run and throw a discus. He can flay, skin, cut up and cook an ox. But all these skills do not explain his eventual success. His secret is that he endures. He accepts what the day brings. He may hunker down, but he never gives in. He takes life as it comes, and that is why he survives.

This trait is so commonly displayed at Boston, it must be

universal. Every human must have this capacity and could find it if he would just put himself in a position to uncover it. There is no better place than a marathon. The truth is that every man in a marathon is a survivor or nothing, including the winner.

Winning is, in fact, little or nothing. "Brief is the season of man's delight," sang Pindar in his ode to an Olympic winner. There is no happy-ever-aftering for a marathoner, no matter what his ability. Tomorrow is another race, another test, another challenge. And when that is done, there is another race, and another.

We aging marathoners already know that. And so when Tennyson has Ulysses speak, we hear ourselves: "And though we are not now the strength which in old days moved earth and heaven, that which we are, we are—made weak by time and fate, but strong in will to strive, to seek, to find and not to yield."

"Not to yield," says it all. The enduring, the surviving does not stop with age. We may even grow more skillful at it as the years pass.

"Though much has been taken," wrote Tennyson, "much abides." Enough and more than enough. We will live and endure. We know, better than others, "how dull it is to pause, to make an end, to rust unburnished, not to shine in use."

I do not intend to pause or rest or rust. Descendant of Ulysses, brother of Bloom, I shall survive.

Part III

THE THINKER

Fifteen

Biggest and Best

"What manner of men are these against whom you have sent us to fight—men who compete in their games not for money, but for honor?"

—Herodotus

Yºu can't say this," Avery Brundage, the world's conscience in amateur sport, once stated, "because people won't understand what you mean. But amateurism is a sort of religion."

Brundage's view of the Promised Land of track and field is the Ancient Greek Olympic Games. They were, he said, "idealistic, semi-religious and amateur." It was only when victory became more important than taking part that the Greeks lost this Eden. Then the Greeks committed at the sins purists like Brundage see happening today: special training camps, recruitment and subsidization of athletes, awarding of prizes and special inducements. The result? The Games degenerated. They lost their purity, their simplicity, their idealism and finally were abolished.

The dogmas of amateurism are being tested now, but it is unlikely that the hierarchy of sport will give in to the demands for change. Facing this formidable opposition is a covey of athletes who would ordinarily be included among the saved. They fill completely Brundage's definition of an amateur: "It is someone who loves, who has devotion to. An amateur athlete is one who loves sport. He works hard and punishes himself and makes the great sacrifices that every athlete has to make because he loves to play and he plays to win because it is fun to win. The professional plays because he's got to win. It's work. It's a job."

Most would-be reformers do not look on track and field as a job. Most do not want to be paid to perform. They want to be permitted to earn enough money to continue in sport, to take care of little items like wives and kids, rent and food. Money, they say, will not influence the true believer. A realistic attitude toward money is all they need.

Their program is simple. Let us, they ask, be permitted to pursue occupations that allow us to take advantage of our name. This is now against AAU rules. No one, for instance, can coach and continue in competition. The apostles of sport and physical fitness fail to see the positive effect on the student body and the track team of a coach who is also an athlete and in good physical condition. Instead, the athlete who is forced out of sport ends up fat, winded and a living indictment of Brundage's true religion.

Point two asks for the continuing eligibility of track athletes who are professionals in other sports. Shot down by present rules are a number of world-class sprinters and hurdlers who play pro football.

Point three is the negotiation with private industry for financial support and sponsoring of meets. This is a sore point with track athletes. Even when they represent the US in international events, they employees continue to view their athletic activities as a hobby and give them no concessions.

The changes in the amateur code aren't going to change athletes' motivations. I suspect the day when money could buy anything, including athletes, has passed. We have a new breed of athletes who understand the social, aesthetic and spiritual aspects of sport. Like the ancient Greeks, they compete not for money but for honor.

A mateurism keeps sports from being part of life," Billie Jean King told a TV interviewer. "It restricts it to those who can afford it."

Earning money, said Billie Jean, can bring back your self-respect. "I was paid under the table and found it very degrading."

That is a strong case for eliminating the amateur status, but there are even stronger ones. The preservation of the idea of amateurism means the preservation of an obsolescent social structure of class and caste.

Professional sports were the province of the slaves in the ancient world and the lower classes in recent centuries. The professional athlete has been the Hessian of sports. The sporting career was accepted only by those who could make their way in society by no other route.

But now we see that sports is no less a profession than any other. There, as in more highly regarded professions, men give of themselves beyond what they are paid. And there, as in other more prestigious professions, men add something above themselves to what they do. There, as in more traditional professions, the only criteria is a person's competence and his standing with his fellows in the game.

The amateur-professional debate, then, is not simply a matter of pay or no pay. It is much bigger than that. The problem is the double standard that protects the man unwilling to invest himself in his game from the man who insists on making the sport his reason for being.

When Frank Shorter, the 1972 Olympic marathon winner, went to his coach Bob Giegengack after three lackluster years at Yale and asked how he could become a good runner, Giegengack had a quick answer: "Give up skiing, drop the undergraduate glee club, eat the right foods and get nine hours of sleep a night." There in one sentence is the difference between the dilettante, the superficial, unengaged, frivolous amateur and the athlete.

"I am a perfectionist," Billie Jean King said. What athlete isn't? What amateur is? To let money determine who will pursue this perfection and who won't is to remain in an age we would prefer to remember for other things than its unthinking acceptance of systems of social caste.

T he discussion of the professional track tour seems to have centered on the question of financial feasibility. On that score, the International Track Association's schedule seems to be an iffy proposition. But the ITA gets high marks in my book for its support of track as a professional activity.

In this age of the amateur, our need for professionals is desperate. Few seem to have the dedication, the know-how, the consistent performance that marks the professional. Too many of us lack the all-consuming interest which is the mark of the pro. Missing is the element of caring which characterizes the professional, be he plumber or pediatrician, lawyer or longshoreman.

We know there is no place in life for the amateur. He is the man unwilling to make that final commitment. And because he is unwilling to put himself on the line, he is always inept, inadequate and uncaring. He excuses himself by minimizing his sport, his work, his profession. It is, he implies, not worth the effort of a man. In the end, he is unwilling or unable to devote himself to any cause—to make anything his full-time pursuit.

We recognize this difference when as spectators we hold professionals accountable. Performance is expected of the professional. When not forthcoming, we feel free to boo him. No one ever boos an amateur. We cheer his effort. We put up with his incompetence. We admire his persistence. But we never boo him, as we could never cut up our daughter's dramatic recitation or our wife's number painting.

So I'm all for runners becoming professionals, although there are some I'm sure who might feel that being a miler is not suitable lifetime ambition, who might be disappointed their son isn't a nuclear physicist instead, who cannot see sports as a profession.

I don't hold with that. We are given our life empty and must be continually occupying it, filling it with what we can do best, specializing in that vocation which fits our body-mind-spirit design. There are some to whom this means being a miler, just as others become third basemen or heart surgeons. For them to know the mile is to know life. Without it, perhaps they would never live completely.

Professional track permits this. It makes possible what was open only to students and servicemen and those subsidized by family or friends—the freedom and time to pursue this vision.

Perhaps the idea of an individual dedicating his life to a quarter-mile track distresses you. It shouldn't. Running is an art and a science. It embodies all we know about the physiology of health and much that we have yet to learn about response to stress. It presents a challenge both physical and psychological and a sense of living at the height of one's powers. It is an excitement at times, a contentment at others.

The runner may learn breathing from an opera singer, flexibility from a ballerina and pace from a racehorse. He may explore the theory of pain, the values of nutrition, the possibilities of psychology, the influence of weather. He may learn about mechanical efficiency from the physicist, about his constitutional strengths and weaknesses from the geneticist and the anthropologist. He will find what all professionals come to know—that the specialist eventually ends up utilizing the knowledge of many other specialists.

Not until a person becomes a professional and accepts the commitment it implies can he begin to realize his potential. Not until a person becomes a professional will his education be more than rapidly-vaporizing subjects. Not until a person becomes a professional will he do anything as if his life depended on it.

Nowadays, they call an athletic scholarship a "grant-in-aid." In my day, an athletic scholarship was called a "free ride."

The *New York Times* once ran exposes on how far a college will go to get an athlete's signature on the dotted line. The Carnegie Commission had already told the country that organized athletics are overshadowing the intellectual life in American universities, and subverting the faculty and students and alumni from their true task.

The Carnegie report is forgotten and will not, I hope, be resurrected. It was based on the intellectuals' mistrust of the body, the idea that learning is of the mind only. The *Times* series will end us as gossip—interesting but of no substance. And the athletic scholarship, the grant-in-aid, the free ride, will continue to be a most necessary fact of college life.

I know. I had one. Unlike the scenarios in the *Times*, the bidding for my services was quite simple. My high school coach, trotted me out to Van Cortlandt Park one day to undergo the scrutiny of Pete Waters, the Manhattan College coach. Later, my coach told me Waters would give me full tuition at Manhattan. This was in 1936 when money was scarce. I went to Manhattan.

I'm not sure to this day what Waters saw in me—except perhaps that I was gaunt and hungry-looking. Whatever it was, I joined a half-dozen who looked exactly like me, and three years later Manhattan had the best cross-country team in the country.

Looking back, I don't remember any soul-searching about receiving free tuition because I was an athlete, any more than I suspect athletes do today. I saw no distinction, for instance, between an academic grant or an athletic one. I had attended high school on an academic scholarship and felt much more comfortable with the athletic one.

If I was a college president, I would be more inclined—based on my own experiences—to give an athletic grant than an academic one. The true scholar tends to withdraw and thinks only of himself and his own little world. He couldn't care less about the college and the rest of the student body. Even this would be acceptable if his path to perfection was visible to his classmates. But his lonely and secret journey never is.

The athlete, on the other hand, pays his way—and not necessarily in gate receipts. He brings excellence in highly visible form to the campus. Never mind that this excellence is in sport, even in a minor sport. Excellence has the same qualities whether it occurs in cross-country or throwing the caber or in nuclear physics. It comes about through discipline and hard work and persistence and reaching back for every source of energy you have hidden away.

This is the answer to the Carnegie Commission question, "What relation does athletics have to an intellectual agency like a university?" Athletics can set a standard of excellence by which every department and every teacher can be judged. Students, once having seen the authentic teacher in the coach and the proper pupil in the athlete, have learned the first great lesson of education: the ability to tell what is first-rate from what is not.

Sport, wrote Baron de Coubertin in his "Ode to Sport," is the delight of the Gods, a distillation of life, a source of beauty, justice, honor, progress and peace. The institutionalization of sport in the modern Olympic Games, he thought, would act to develop character and sportsmanship—something to be desired by every citizen.

Despite the events at Munich, I believe he was correct. The tragedy and the trivia of the Olympics there does not dissuade me from this view. Nor can critics convince me that the Olympics have somehow forfeited their place in society. The Olympics are and will remain one of the great social forces in the world.

"Few who have been touched by the spirit of the Olympics can forget it," writes Professor Howell Maxwell. "It leaves a mark on all who have experienced its magic."

That magic, the critics would have us believe, was missing at Munich. I doubt it. We had, if anything, the greatest athletic meets ever held. In men's track, three of the most challenging events on the program—the intermediate hurdles, the 10,000 meters and the decathlon—were won in world record performances. Lyudmila Bragina lowered the women's 1500-meter record three straight times.

Make no mistake. Athletes around the world had done their homework for this meet. They honored the Olympics by their feats of speed and skill and strength and endurance. Behind each of the record setters were hundreds and thousands like them, enduring denial and deprivation and pain and fatigue in their pursuit of Olympic gold.

Where, then, did the Olympics fail? The records were there, the competence and beauty of the athletes that brought a lump to your throat, a tear to your eye. What was the big complaint? A coach who misread the schedule? A silly argument about a pole?

Of course not. These are trivia. It was the tragedy—the intrusion of the men of Black September, leaving five of their own, 11 Israelis and a West German dead. How could anyone play games then? "Wasn't it time," asked Red Smith in the *New York Times*, "to put away the sand box?"

But the Games did go on. They went on because this bitter, murderous violence is exactly why we need Olympic Games. And we will continue to need the Olympics until we can accept the definition of a hero as one who is willing to die for a cause but not to kill for it.

Mourning the victims of these bloody quarrels should not deviate us, or the athletes, or those crotchety old men in the International Olympic Committee from our common cause— peace and brotherhood.

"Our aim," said Avery Brundage as he was packing to leave the IOC, "is to set standards: standards of decency, standards of sport and standards of life."

The Olympics have fulfilled that aim. They have become an institution, and like all institutions they reflect the society in which they exist. Materialism, greed, nationalism, incompetence, whatever characterizes our society must be seen to some extent in the Olympics. But since it is an institution with high ideals and standards, it has also suggested and even precipitated significant advances in our society.

This is the natural outcome of the continual upgrading of standards of decency, sport and life. If goals thought to be physically impossible are continually surpassed in sport, why then can't we do the same things thought socially or politically impossible? Why should we allow war and violence and discrimination to exist?

And what about our abnormal nationalism? Isn't it time to remove the flags and strip the anthems? Aren't we beyond adding up each country's loot in medals and honors? Maybe, but not yet. Each tribe, each nation adds to the human experience, increases the human possibility. It is right to bring something of what Robert Lipstye calls "birth and breed and border" to this giant convocation of the human clan. We still need to know where we came from and who came with us. What we don't need are anthems filled with war and killing, stirring passions hardly reconcilable with de Coubertin's ideas of sport and beauty and peace.

There are men in the United States (and I include myself) who find the words "the rockets' red glare, the bombs bursting in air" quite hard to stomach. Yet these same people may stand wet-eyed and transported during "America, the Beautiful" or "This Land is My Land." Is it too much to hope that the anthems, but not the flags or the ceremonies, will be changed when we reach Montreal in 1976 or Moscow in 1980?

Mankind," wrote Pierre Teilhard de Chardin, "is braced together in an effort to discover. And what does it seek to discover if not ultimately to super-, or at least to ultra-hominise itself." Hominise is a Teilhardian word for a human prolonged beyond itself in a better organized, more adult form.

Now this is pretty heavy going for this child of *Psychology Today* and *Sports Illustrated*. But I suspect he's right. In fact, the Olympics tells me he's right. Man, says the Munich Olympics, is born to be a winner. He is born to be super- or at least ultra-hominised. The athletes I watched there convinced me it's so.

Let those pessimists about man's future look to the Olympics. Let those who think humanity is slipping backwards contemplate the ultimate becoming commonplace and new records, new ultimates, new heights of performance occurring every four years. And let those who despair of this generation watch this harvest of Americans and Japanese and Russians and Germans and Brazilians and Kenyans who are on their way to becoming household heroes not nationally but internationally.

The Olympic imperative of *Citius, Altius, Fortius* (swifter, higher, stronger) has become part of the lives of these competitors. They have preserved in their heart and mind a passion for growth. They seek not so much to enjoy more or to know more but to *be* more.

All this should have an effect, should raise our sights to our own possibilities, should make us see that the Olympic year is not just for Olympic stars but for all of us who try to fulfill ourselves. The Olympic ideal is addressed to everyone.

Those of us who have long since left our childhood should not lose faith. "Wait until next year" is no hollow threat in the field of physical fitness or athletic endeavor. Twelve months can transform a lounge lizard into a physiological marvel. Three hundred sixty-five days can convert a basket case from booze, butts and baked goods into an endurance phenomenon.

And this is not merely subjective improvement, not simply a case of "feeling good" or having a "zest for living" or possessing "loads of energy." This physical change is measurable by stopwatch and tape, oxygen capacity, muscle strength and muscle skills.

The improvement of Olympic records is a reflection of the improvements in technique, training, muscle development, diet and general regimen over the years. The meet is, in effect, a huge international fair of human husbandry (although no such field exists) where the best of everything that has been discovered in the field of human development and human potential is put to the crucial test.

Here we can learn under the accelerated and compressed circumstances of all-out, highest-level athletic competition what works and what doesn't.

No wonder Pope Paul said that the sight of these strong, healthy and agile youths had reawakened in him "the hope of a new world based on fraternity and order" and that he had found in sport "an encouragement to the fullness of man, which makes him seek a perfection which goes beyond that which is merely physical."

Sixteen

Work and Play

To play or not to play? That is the real question. Shakespeare was wrong. Anyone with a sense of humor can see that life is a joke, not a tragedy. It is a riddle and like all riddles has an obvious answer: play, not suicide.

Think about it for a minute. Is there a better way to handle "the slings of and arrows of outrageous fortune" or take up arms against "a sea of troubles" than play? You take these things seriously and you end up with Hamlet or the gang who came back from World War II, wrote Wilfred Sheed, "talking about dollars the way others talked of God and sex."

Neither of these ways work. Neither will bring us what we are supposed to be looking for, "the peace the world cannot give." That is also part of the riddle. You can have peace without the world, if you opt for death, or the world without peace if you decide for doing and having and achieving. Only in play can you have both.

In play you realize simultaneously the supreme importance and the utter insignificance of what you are doing. You accept the paradox of pursuing what is at once essential and inconsequential. In play you can totally commit yourself to a goal that minutes later is completely forgotten.

Play, then, is the answer to the puzzle of our existence, the stage for our excesses and exuberances. Violence and dissent are part of its joy. Territory is defended with every ounce of our strength and determination, and moments later we are embracing our opponents and delighting in the game that took place.

Play is where life lives, where the game is the game. At its borders, we slip into heresy, become serious, lose our sense of humor, fail to see the incongruities of everything we hold to be important. Right and wrong become problematical. Money, power, position become ends. The game becomes winning. And we lose the good life and the good things that play provides.

If the common man has erred in this century, it is in his failure to realize the importance of play. The aristocracy never made that mistake. Aristocrats know that work is a luxury and play is a necessity of life. When money and position give the freedom to pursue the good life, work is seen to be a diversion, a distraction from the most basic and the most—to use Maslow's word—actualizing human activity, play.

We are slowly awakening to this truth. Teachers now see the ideal learning environment is the environment of children at play. Physical education is being revived by bringing play back into its curriculum. Health and fitness, every medical journal is telling us, comes only to those who play hard and often.

And finally the theologians, always the last to learn, are starting to ask themselves if play might not be the primary activity of man. Theologian Gabriel Moran has called play, "one of the most intriguing and potentially fruitful interests of contemporary theology." Certainly, a case can be made that the true object of life is play.

Plato spoke of man as "God's plaything" and urged everyone to "make the noblest games the real content of their lives." And in Proverbs we read, "His delight was in playing with the children of men."

We have missed the point of all this because we have not understood play. It is not, as we believed, simply a method of

relieving tension and providing relaxation. Nor is it a service activity preparing us for the more serious and important everyday
world, the real world.

Play, as the true player knows, is the most real thing that
he does. Indeed, one must play with a passionate involvement,
play as if his life depended on it, if play is to mean anything at
all.

One man's play can, of course, be another man's boredom.
Anyone reading the Lawrence Shainberg article on Frank
Shorter in the *New York Times Magazine* would realize that.
Shorter's idea of play is running 22 miles a day at a six-minutes-
per-mile clip, occasionally interspersing these tortures with a
series of agonizing interval quarter-mile runs. And the whole
joyful routine ends in a marathon where he has to "redline"
(maintain as long as possible the fastest pace one's body can
bear) and "go it on mind alone" (the task that confronts a runner when he has superseded the normal limits of his body).

Yet there can be no doubt this mixture of pain and pleasure is play. It exists of and by itself and serves no utilitarian
purpose. Why does he do it? "There's always the feeling of getting stronger," Shorter told Shainberg. "I think that's what
keeps me going."

That explanation may be inadequate for some, but for
me it contains enough theological implications for a doctoral
thesis. Strong is Anglo-Saxon for what the Romans called
virtus, and from this Latin root comes man and virtue. The
growing strength that Shorter feels is obviously as spiritual
and intellectual as it is physical.

Shorter belongs to that group of people that William
James said resent confusion and must have purity, consis-
tency and simplicity. The marathoner is by most standards a peculiar guy. He has found freedom through the acceptance of
rules, has cured his loneliness with solitude and has discovered
the peace inside of pain. He is a blood brother to another
peculiar guy, Henry David Thoreau, who spoke of his play
(walking) in this way:

"If you are ready to leave father and mother, and brother

and sister, and wife and children and friends, and never see them again—if you have paid your debts and made your will and settled all your affairs and are a free man, then you are ready for a walk."

Even for the free man, life is a dangerous and difficult game. Man, the player, must train long and hard before he can move through life with the simple, certain, leisurely grace of the expert. Still, it is the only game in town.

That sport would be put under the microscope, analyzed and criticized was inevitable. We are living in an age when every human activity, every institution is coming under scrutiny, being evaluated, having to prove its reason for existence. The important thing for the athlete to do is not to take this outpouring too seriously, not to apply the generalizations of the philosophers, the psychologists, the sociologists to his own living of the athletic life.

The warning may be unnecessary. When one becomes a true believer, no argument, no rationalizations, no accumulation of facts is going to turn him away from his faith. But for those not yet convinced, institutionalized sport can be a stumbling block. Concentration on the past, failure to move with the times, authoritarianism and an excessive legalism can cause a man to quit a locker room as quickly as a cathedral.

We must distinguish what is primary in sport from what are its aberrations, what is essential to sport and what it is equally essential to eliminate or ignore.

The approach to take to sport, it seems to me, is the approach William James took to religion. "I wrote this book (*The Varieties of Religious Experience*)," he told a friend, "to make the reader believe that although all the special manifestations of religion may have been absurd, the life of it as a whole is mankind's most important function." The real backbone of the religious life, said James, was experience, not philosophy. No philosophy of religion, he contended, could begin to be an adequate translation of what goes on in the single private man.

Could you find any better antidote to the intellectuals' attempts to rationalize you at play, give you motives for athletics, provide a reward for your sport? Sport defies their explanations. Man playing is almost as difficult a subject as man praying.

"I think, therefore I am" is the philosophy of the incomplete man.

"We are happy," writes David Cole Gordon, "when, however briefly, we become one with ourselves, others and the world of nature." Sport certainly provides such moments. The fact that they mostly defy description may cause outsiders and observers to doubt their existence. But all athletes know the truth of "I play, therefore I am."

Some of the good things in play are physical grace, phychological ease and personal integrity. The best are the peak experiences, when you have a sense of oneness with yourself and nature. These are truly times of peace the world cannot give. It may be that the hereafter will have them in constant supply. I hope so. But while we are in the here and now, play is the place to find them—the place where we are constantly being and becoming ourselves.

Philosophers have hinted at this over the centuries. Now theologians are taking a hard look at the thought that we must become as little children to enter the Kingdom. If so, there is nothing more characteristic about children than their love of play. No one comes into this world a Puritan. If there is anything children care less about, it is work and money and power and what we call achievement. They live in love and security and acceptance. Nowhere in their world is the need to prove their right to exist, the necessity to be a success.

What happened to our play on our way to becoming adults? Downgraded by the intellectuals, dismissed by the economists, put aside by the psychologists, it was left to the teachers to deliver the *coup de grace*. Physical education was born and turned what was joy into boredom, what was fun into drudgery, what was pleasure into work. What might have led us into Eden led us into a blind alley instead.

Play, of course, says otherwise. You may already have found that out. If you are doing something you would do for nothing, then you are on your way to salvation. And if while you are doing it you are transported into another existence, there is no need for you to worry about the future.

In his "Assignment Sports," *New York Times* sports columnist Bob Lipsyte expresses his disappointment with people who ask him, "What are you going to do when you grow up?"

"Anyone who says that," claims Lipsyte, "is not too smart. Politics, religion, money, the law all play roles in sports. The world of sports is no sanctuary from reality."

Lipsyte is, of course, right on. I suspect that, more often than not, politics, religion, money and the law are the real sanctuaries from reality, whereas sport is an immediate, engrossing human experience which involves man in his wholeness, completely realized in all his aspects.

Take the long distance runner. Here is the object of a phrase "the loneliness of the long distance runner," which in many ways encapsulates all our false notions about sports. The lonely long distance runner stands for "my husband, the nut," or "my roomate, the character," or "my brother, the misfit." He raises an image of some oddball who has confused his priorities and has settled into a permanent semi-adolescent state of isolation, unable to rise above the level of play and games.

Try again. Smith, the runner in that novel by Alan Sillitoe, was lonely only when he *wasn't* running. "Sometimes," he said, "I think I've never been as free as during that couple of hours when I'm trotting up the path." There is no hint, you see, that his loneliness was part of his distance running. It may well, if we read his words correctly, have been the cure.

Thoreau had already spoken to us of the cure to be found in solitude. Thoreau was not lonely. He described himself when he described the sparrow hawk. "It appeared to have no companion in the universe and to need none but the morning. It was not lonely but it made all the world lonely beneath it."

Like the soaring hawk, Smith finds his freedom—his escape from the loneliness of the reform school—in his running. Only when his running becomes a source of prestige and gratification to the superintendent, when he realizes he is being manipulated, when his sport is being used in the "real" world, does his loneliness again intrude on him. Not the running but society thrusts him back into the lonely shell he had occupied.

Society, if we can believe sociologist Philip Slater, is presently engaged in thrusting all of us into a state of loneliness. Only Slater in his brilliant, bitter and often despairing book, *The Pursuit of Loneliness*, says we go there willingly and knowingly, carried along by our belief in the scarcity principle—the assumption that the world does not contain enough wherewithal to satisfy the needs of its human inhabitants.

Hence, Americans seek competition instead of community, and uninvolvement rather than engagement with social and interpersonal problems. The result, writes Slater, is that the returning traveler re-entering the United States is struck by the fanatical acquisitiveness of his compatriots. "It is difficult," he says, "to become reaccustomed to seeing people already weighed down with possessions acting as if every object they did not own were bread withheld from a hungry mouth."

Another sociologist, Dr. Whitney Gordon, found something similar in a study of Muncie, Ind. Muncie's predominant social values, he reported, were the importance of work, of enterprise, of upward mobility, of material rewards. " 'Making it' for the worker after the two cars is the color TV, and if he has that, a camper is a status symbol," says Gordon. " 'Making it' in the upper income groups is membership in the country club, travel abroad or a Cadillac."

If that is reality, the long distance runner may indeed be seeking sanctuary from it. There is no scarcity principle in running. All can share without in any way diminishing the other. It is moreover a universal language understood by all men, an endeavor in which all men can relate and instantly be brothers.

"Sports brings out," writes artist-photographer Robert Riger, "the classic greatness and dignity of man. In the struggle and in the race there is an almost divine accord of beauty and grace."

Can a plodder feel all this? Better, it's my guess, than any politician, cleric, businessman or lawyer. What are they going to do when *they* grow up?

One plus the intellectuals give sport is its role in working off aggression and violence. It is, they tell us, one of those "moral equivalents of war" that William James said was so necessary. Championship bouts, Super Bowls, World Series, the Olympic Games all give us the opportunity to discharge our natural pugnacity. They provide safe outlets for the sadism and hate that seem to well up in us.

This concession is right as far as it goes. But it is incomplete. James also saw war as a school for the strenuous life and for heroism. It is a setting in which a man found he could withstand unimaginable hardships. It was a theater in which a man found depths of energy and endurance he never knew he possessed.

What James sought was not simply an alternative to violence, but some other human activity or life-style that would unleash man's marvelous hidden energies. Athletics, he thought, could bring out these enormous subterranean resources without demanding that the athlete give up his moral notions. Sport could give us our chance for the strenuous life, let us experience the heroic, allow us to transform our military courage.

This is a long way from the dissipation of violence. It has to do with the way a life should be lived. Like Tolstoy, James was dismayed by the cerebral life—the life of conventionality, artificiality and personal ambition. Like Ortega, he came unstuck when he saw lives without purpose or project.

People outside of sport may only see the game, just as those outside of war only see the horror. Yet, in that horror a man may be better than he will ever be the rest of his life. And in that game a man may find what life is really all about. It is more likely that the critics are the ones who are living a life

that is a game. Intricate and bright and clever, perhaps, but a game. They are only simulating life.

In sport, there is no such dalliance. The athlete is Ortega's "noble man." He always demands more of himself, lives under bondage to self-imposed tasks and imperatives and devotes his life to collaboration with others. He does this because he must, because sport exposes any less effort and throws a bright light on any failure of nerve.

But sport allows more than that. It allows for redemption. Everything is possible. You continually make your own life.

The gut issue in the United States today," writes Tom Wicker, the *New York Times* columnist, "is the lack of quality from top to bottom in American life." Wicker's plaint about appliances that don't work, streets that are not cleaned, laws that are not enforced, and the general feeling that people either do not know or care about their work is not new.

The same problem was the theme of the McCarthy campaign in 1968 when he appealed for a revived sense of profession and vocation in modern society.

Now Cornell professor Andrew Hacker suggests that it may be too late. America, says Hacker, is going to hell in a wheelbarrow and there's not much we can do about it. He bases his prognosis on our refusal to accept authority, a contempt for government and the loss of a moral consensus. "America's history as a nation," concludes Hacker, "has reached its end."

Wicker, Hacker and a multitude of critics, journalists, sociologists and other observers may be right, but I suspect you may find the same thoughts in a recently excavated Egyptian papyrus and the collected works of Plato. The world has always been going to hell in a wheelbarrow.

That it doesn't is because there are always men who lead us into the future. A few are astronauts, some are scientists, many are artists, a number are athletes, none are politicians. And of these men, the athlete is the most heroic.

"Athletes are important," writes British novelist Brian

Glanville, "because they demonstrate the scope of human possibility, which is unlimited. The inconceivable is conceived and then it is accomplished." They, perhaps more obviously than other men, fit Thoreau's description when he wrote, "Some record only what happened to them but others how *they* happened to the universe."

Bilke wrote, "People are wrong about the motion of the future. The future stands still. It is we who are moving in infinite space." Which makes the gut issue in the United States today, when are we going to get off our butts?

We are constantly being warned to check with our physicians before beginning athletics. Play and games evidently can be risky business. What we are not told are the risks of *not* beginning athletics—that the most dangerous sport of all is watching it from the stands.

The weakest among us can become some kind of athlete, but only the strongest can survive as spectators. Only the hardiest can withstand the perils of inertia, inactivity and immobility. Only the most resilient can cope with the squandering of time, the deterioration in fitness, the loss of creativity, the frustration of the emotions and the dulling of moral sense that can afflict the dedicated spectator.

Physiologists have suggested that only those who can pass the most rigorous physical examination can safely follow the sedentary life. Man was not made to remain at rest. Inactivity is completely unnatural to the body. And what follows is a breakdown of the body's equilibrium.

When the beneficial effects of activity on the heart and circulation and indeed on all the body's systems are absent, everything measurable begins to go awry. Up goes the girth of the waist and the body weight. Up goes blood pressure and heart rate. Up goes cholesterol and triglycerides. Up goes everything you would like to go down and down goes everything you would like to go up. Down goes vital capacity and oxygen consumption. Down goes flexibility and efficiency, stamina and strength. Fitness fast becomes a memory.

The seated spectator is not a thinker, he is a knower. Unlike the athlete who is still seeking his own experience, who leaves himself open to truth, the spectator has closed the ring. His thinking has become rigid knowing. He has enclosed himself in bias and partisanship and prejudice. He has ceased to grow.

And it is growth he needs most to handle the emotions thrust upon him, emotions he cannot act out in any satisfactory way. He is, you see, an incurable distance from the athlete and participation in the effort that is the athlete's release, the athlete's catharsis. He is watching people who have everything he wants and cannot get. They are having all the fun: the fun of playing, the fun of winning, even the fun of losing. They are having the physical exhaustion which is the quickest way to fraternity and equality, the exhaustion which permits you to be not only a good winner but a good loser.

Because the spectator cannot experience what the athlete is experiencing, the fan is seldom a good loser. The emphais on winning is therefore much more of a problem for the spectator than the athlete. The losing fan, filled with emotions which have no healthy outlets, is likely to take it out on his neighbor, the nearest inanimate object, the umpires, the stadium or the game itself. It is easier to dry out a drunk, take someone off hard drugs or watch a three-pack-a-day man go cold turkey than live with a fan during a long losing streak.

Should a spectator pass all these physical and mental and emotional tests, he still has another supreme challenge to his integrity. He is part of a crowd, part of a mob. He is one with those the coach in *The Games* called, "The nothingmen, those oafs in the stands filling their bellies." And when someone is in a crowd, out go his individual standards of conduct and morality. He acts in concert with his fellow spectators and descends two or three rungs on the evolutionary ladder. He slips backward down the developmental tree.

From the moment you become a spectator, everything is downhill.

Seventeen

Questions and Answers

Is happiness a five-mile fix? Are those runners we see on the roads these early mornings and late evenings there in pursuit of the life, liberty and happiness the Declaration of Independence said was the right of all men?

The answer, according to Edwin Land, the genius who heads the Polaroid Corporation, is probably yes. "Addiction," says Land, "is a necessity and an opportunity." And distance running is clearly an addiction of major proportions.

Land's particular obsession is not running but scientific experiment. Unless he performs one good experiment a day, "the world goes out of focus, becomes unreal."

Land came to realize the universal nature of addiction when he discussed his reaction to the scientific experience at a university seminar. After hearing the recital of an experiment's sequence of intuition, mystery, excitement and the final relief and nobility, a bearded youth in the front row turned to a companion and said, "Why, it's just like heroin, isn't it?"

You don't have to tell a genius more than once. Land pounced on the idea and came up with one of the more sensible statements made on the drug problem in memory. Scientific experiment, he reasoned, must be an addiction and must do what heroin is trying to do, but constructively.

The addict is not escaping from reality but is trying to find himself. Runners are doing the same thing, but in a constructive, continually satisfying and maturing way.

Running's addictive qualities are unquestioned. Doug Hardin, former Harvard cross-country captain, once said that his daily workouts regulate his whole life—his eating habits, his social schedule and his academic future. And why not? "They ranged," he said, "from deepest drama to mere routine, keen excitement to utter boredom, great sensual pleasure to extreme agony." Hardin himself considered distance running not as a sport but "an obsession."

This obsession with running is really an obsession with the potential for more and more life.

W hen it's pouring with rain and you're bowling along through the wet," said Peter Snell about running, "there's a satisfaction of knowing you're out there and the others aren't."

Runners are wondering whether that satisfaction is enough. Their sport has survived charges that it is dangerous. (Dr. Harry Johnson of the Life Extension Institute found that 29 out of 30 cardiologists in his survey recommended against jogging for sedentary men over 50), boring (the *New Yorker* has called it a "pastime of overpowering ennui") and ineffectual (the American Medical Association says the "burden of proof still rests with those who state that jogging will prevent coronary disease").

Now they are being told jogging is safe, interesting and effective—but unnecessary. It can be replaced by something as simple as hypnosis or hatha yoga.

Canadian physicians divided their post-coronary heart patients into two groups. One group was given a program of daily jogging and exercise. The other was put into the hands of psychiatrist E. Harvey Doney (himself a heart victim who practices self-hypnosis), who induced the patients into a hypnotic trance. They imagined themselves jogging or pictured themselves in a beautiful meadow filling their lungs with wonderful fresh air and "feeling the oxygen going through the whole body reaching the heart."

The results after a year? Identical improvement in both groups. Weight and body fat down, increase in grip strength and EKG tracings, lowering of blood pressure and lessening of the adrenalin production by the body.

Should these findings shake joggers down to their arch supports? Of course not. If they keep their cool they can see what all this means.

It means, for one thing, that heart disease and nervous tension are intimately connected. John Hunter, who first described coronary disease and was himself a sufferer, wrote, "I am at the mercy of any fool who can aggravate me." This notion of stress and irritation was echoed recently by a leading German heart specialist, Berthold Kern. Kern blames "agitation and aggravation"—and not obesity, excessive cigarette smoking and high cholesterol—for heart attacks.

The Canadian study also suggests that there are a variety of ways of relaxing and overcoming feelings of tension—of which jogging is only one. One alternate method that comes to mind is hatha yoga. And we may be in for a revival of hypnosis and yoga in the sports and fitness fields.

Hatha yoga was over a thousand years old when it burst on the sports scene in the person of Lou Nova, poet and heavyweight boxer. It was an inauspicious start. Nova blew in from California with his yoga exercises and his "cosmic punch." He was, said the west coast scribes, a cinch to take Joe Louis and join the immortals. They were right in one respect—Nova did attain immortality. He became the first and only man to make Louis smile. His cosmic punch missed by so much it broke the Brown Bomber up. . .but only temporarily as Louis soon had the poet in a prolonged meditative pose on the canvas.

Yoga has since surfaced to better press in the form of mini-yoga, said to be the secret of skier Jean-Claude Killy and his French teammates. "You cannot win races," said Killy, "if you are not relaxed." And under the direction of coach Honore Bonnet the French skiers did 30 minutes of yoga exercises a day. The object: keep the mind loose and the body limber. "The purpose," explained Bonnet, "is to liberate the mind and relax the body."

Hypnosis aims for the same thing. The emphasis is always on relaxed physical and mental well-being: bolstering the patient's confidence and stressing his capabilities. "It is best suited for handling excessive emotional tension in patients," says psychiatrist Lewis Wolberg of the New York Medical College, and adds, "It has never gained the acceptance it deserves as a meritorious adjunct in medicine."

The key word is adjunct—to be used with physical exercise—not in place of it. The runner can be assured that hypnosis alone will not make him fit or allow him to do endurance efforts without fatigue. But he should also know that 30 minutes of running, three times a week, is sufficient for conditioning—if not competition.

Why then must joggers go out almost every day for their 3-5-mile jaunts? Obviously, say the yoga and hypnosis enthusiasts, because they are addicts, mainliners, and this trip is a *trip.* . . .

I think the first one who said that virtue could not be taught was Socrates. It's still news, however, to the daily press which made a minor furor about an article in *Psychology Today* called "Sport: If You Want to Build Character, Try Something Else." The fact that the authors, San Jose State psychologists Bruce Olgivie and Thomas Tutko, are consultants for 27 professional teams in basketball, football, ice hockey and golf, and have worked with hundreds of high school and college teams in every major sport should have alerted the journalists to read their conclusions more carefully.

They didn't, and the country got the impression that the Ogilvie and Tutko opus was anti-sport. It isn't, except for that catchy title. What they state is that sports may not build character (because nothing will and we're not sure, anyway, that we want to), but it can make happy, fulfilled people. This is what most of us are searching for now: exploring our possibilities, trying to become the thing we are.

A close reading of the essay will show Ogilvie and Tutko have nothing but good things to say about sport. The following few quotes will put this conclusion in the proper perspective:

● *"Athletic competition has no more beneficial effect than intense endeavor in any other field."*

It is, however, one of the few fields into which people will put such intense endeavor. A fortunate few, points out philosopher Paul Weiss, carry an intense interest in their prime activity into their leisure time. Among them are the athlete, the artist, the scientist, the politician and the man of religion.

● *"The competitive sports experience is unique in the way it compresses the selection process into a compact time and space. The young athlete must face in a few hours the kind of pressure that occurs in the life of an achievement-oriented man over several years."*

Sport has this tremendous potential for self-revelation. What we want to know is who we are. Sport can tell us as quickly, painlessly and as surely as any other human activity. Where else can we risk failure and defeat without the great fear that it will be irrevocable?

● *"The rapidity and clarity of the feedback in competitive sport provide a fine opportunity for the individual athlete who knows which traits he wants to change and who has the motivation to do so."*

And this article was supposed to be against sports? Our psychologist friends are telling us that here, par excellence, is the learning situation. Here is a laboratory of life where one can pursue maturity without psychological hazard.

● *"The new direction in athletics will be toward helping athletes make personally chosen modifications in behavior; toward the joyous pursuit of esthetic experience; toward a wide variety of personality types and values."*

Ogilvie and Tutko are revealing their true colors. They are sports fans and enthusiasts from the tip of their Freudian toes to the roots of their Jungian hair. The title was just a ploy—a Trojan Horse to get into the camp of the enemy. Sport will not build character; it will do something better. It will make a man free.

The free man is not what you or society want him to be. He wears no mask. He is the total expression of his body-mind-soul relationship—and nothing else, or he would be false. Sport, says Ogilvie and Tutko, can help you find that fully functioning person your whole being wants you to be.

Tom Tutko specializes in sports psychology and marriage counseling—two areas where pretense and masks will never work. "I am the original frustrated jock," he says. "I would like to play ball the rest of my life. Unfortunately, I have the motivation but not the talent."

This deficiency won't stop either him or us. Talent or not, character and virtue be damned, sport will continue to reveal each man to himself and to his brother.

A rnold Burns is not an athlete or an artist, scientist or politician. He is a garment district executive, and a fictitious one at that. He exists only in the play, "A Thousand Clowns," where he seems to be all the Romans meant when they coined the word "mediocre," one who is midway up the hill.

Burns is a middle-class man handcuffed by the middle-class responsibilities of a middle-class family, living out a middle-class life. He is everything the sociologists wring their hands over—the American male caught in a mesh of worries, still dreaming the really impossible dream.

But Arnold Burns sees it differently. "You don't respect me so much," he tells his brother, the unhappy intellectual. "You want to be a hero. . .I'm willing to deal with the available world. . .I'm not an exceptional man and I have a talent for surrender. I'm at peace. I'm not one of the bad guys. I take pride." And then in summation, he states, "I am the best possible Arnold Burns."

Mediocrity, you see, is in the eye of the beholder. Arnold

Burns is not halfway up anybody's mountain. He is at the top of his own. He is the king of his hill. Anyone can be a success, he tells us, unless he tries to climb someone else's mountain. Man, no matter how mediocre he appears, is still the greatest wonder in the world.

Burns agrees with Bucky Fuller. Man is born to be a success. There are no failures in nature. Failure occurs when our goals are unrealistic, false and too vague, when we have no idea who we are or where we are going.

The key then is to find your own mountain. Otherwise, you will be competing with people who are not even in your event, and running up against the "shoulds" and "oughts" of that world, and the inevitable frustration and depression and feelings of failure. A person can be complete or incomplete, but one thing is sure: he cannot be someone else.

Arnold Burns knows the someone-he-is to be the butt of the jokes of the intellectuals and the academic world, much the same way as men of action, the game-playing jocks, are looked upon as deviants from man's perfection.

The truth is that there is no such one perfect man or woman. Each of us is able to be the best possible unique person we are—and no other.

What is primary, however, is not the desire to be different or peculiar, but to have that difference, that originality, derive from a course of action natural to your body-mind-spirit totality—the unique person you are. If this person fails to meet the criteria of virtue and achievement and righteousness that other segments of the society have agreed upon, so be it.

Arnold Burns, who is one such original, is telling me that, unlikely as it seems, his life is a masterpiece. And, therefore, unlikely as it seems, mine and yours can be one, too.

Where have all the heroes gone?" asked novelist Edward Hoagland in the *New York Times Magazine*. And his question taken up a day or two later by sports writer Bob Lipsyte.

"Help! Wanted: Hero or Heroine" was the name of the Lipsyte piece.

Both pointed out that the traditional heroes no longer held our respect or admiration. Hoagland observed that experts and physicians, soldiers and statesmen aren't heroes to anyone at the present time. And Lipsyte saw no one in the soldier-statesman-athlete pool who could fill Carlyle's definition of the heroic man: the messenger sent from the infinite unknown with tidings for all of us. There seemed to be no one ready to seize fire and run with it.

In Hoagland's view, the hero has died from familiarity. "One must love one's heroes," he wrote, "notwithstanding their pains, self-doubts and inconsistencies—which is much more difficult with overexposure."

There you have it. The transistor did them in. TV and the electronic age have freed future generations from the cult of these public successes and private failures. Our communication marvels have shown us that heroes not only have feet of clay, they have lives of clay. This has given us a clue to who are the real winners and losers in this world. More than anything else, we have come to see the hero as a man simply trying to become what he conceives himself to be.

We know that the major battles in life are waged unseen and unnoticed. We the people truly dream the impossible dream, fight the unbeatable foe and bear unbearable sorrows. We are on that quest, no matter how hopeless, no matter how far. And we know it is only in pursuing that quest that we will finally come to rest fulfilled.

So we are all heroes to some degree. We become more so as we base our actions on ourselves and ourselves alone. "Heroism," wrote Ortega, "is the will to be oneself." The hero's will is not that of family or custom or society, but his own. His life is a resistance to what is customary and habitual, to business as usual. The hero takes himself and his place in time and creates his own drama.

Hear Ortega again on this. We come into this world, he

says, to play a part for which neither script nor role has been established. It is for us to compose and act out the drama of our existence. No one else can or should do this for us. There is no hero, past or future, who can be used as a model.

Where have all the heroes gone? They've gone with the simplicities and the pieties and the easy answers of another era. Our lack of heroes is an indication of the maturity of our age—a realization that everyman has come into his own and has the capability of making a success out of his life. Success rests with having the courage and endurance and, above all, the will to become the person you are, however peculiar that may be.

Then you will be able to say, "I have found my hero and he is me."

About the Author

George Sheehan was born in Brooklyn on Nov. 5, 1918, and educated in city schools. He attended Manhattan College where he was a member of the 1938 and 1939 IC4A championship cross-country team. In 1940, he was runner-up in the IC4A indoor mile to Leslie MacMitchell. Subsequently, George went to the Long Island College of Medicine, interned in the US Navy and had a residency in medicine at Kings County Hospital in Brooklyn.

In 1949, he began private practice in Red Bank, N.J. He has continued there since and is at the present time Head of the Department of Electrocardiography and Stress Testing at Riverview Hospital.

Previously occupied with tennis and squash, he began running again at the age of 44, and since then has missed training on the roads only because of illness or injury. He runs about 30 miles a week, competes regularly at distances from the half-mile to the marathon and has completed the last 12 Boston Marathons. At the age of 50, he ran a 4:47.6 mile which was then a world's record for that age-group.

In 1968, Sheehan began a weekly column for the *Red Bank Daily Register* under the title "The Innocent Bystander." In 1970, he started a medical advice column in *Runner's World* and in 1972 became Medical Editor. That year, World Publications issued his first book, *Encyclopedia of Athletic Medicine.*

In 1974, he became a columnist with *The Physician & Sportsmedicine* with a monthly column called "Running Wild."

George is married to the former Mary Jane Fleming. They live in Rumson, N.J., in a large old rambling house which serves as home base for their 12 children.